# The Ultimate Guide for Turning Code into Cash

## From Idea to Income

*Tommy Burke*

# Copyrights

This book is a work of non-fiction. The information contained within is based on research and factual information, and any opinions expressed are the author's own.

Cover design by Tommy Burke

Tommy C. Burke
Apollo Beach, FL
https://www.tcburke314.com/

ISBN: 9798372879614
Imprint: Independently published

 First edition: January 2023

# Disclaimers & Notices

## LEGAL DISCLAIMER

This book contains many templates for various business and legal documents. Each of these are free for you to use at your discretion. However, this book is not intended to provide legal advice. The information contained in this book is for general informational purposes only and is not intended to be a substitute for professional legal advice. The information provided in this book is based on the author's research and understanding of the topic, and the author is not a lawyer or legal professional. The author does not warrant the completeness or accuracy of the information contained in this book. You should seek the advice of a qualified lawyer or legal professional before relying on any information contained in this book.

## BUSINESS DISCLAIMER

The information contained in this book is based on the author's research and understanding of the topic and is presented as a technical guide for accomplishing the topics discussed. While the author has made every effort to ensure the accuracy and completeness of the information contained in this book, the author cannot guarantee the accuracy or completeness of the information. You should not rely on the information contained in this book as a substitute for professional advice or expertise.

## NON-ENDORSEMENT DISCLAIMER

The mention of specific companies, products, software platforms, and websites in this book does not constitute an endorsement or recommendation by the author or publisher. The author has no affiliation with any of the companies or organizations mentioned in this book, and the inclusion of these companies, products, software platforms, and websites in this book does not imply endorsement or recommendation by the author or publisher. The author is not advocating for any particular products or companies, and the views expressed in this book are the author's own and do not reflect the views of any of the companies or organizations mentioned in this book.

## ATTRIBUTION

In creating this book, I used OpenAI's GPT-3 large-scale language-generation model for assistance in refining my outline, ensuring the completeness of concepts, and attempting to provide a well-rounded and comprehensive guide. This allowed me to refine my own ideas around certain topics and determine starting points for additional research. As such, it should be understood that:

I, the author, generated this text in part with GPT-3, OpenAI's large-scale language-generation model. Upon generating draft language, I reviewed, edited, and revised the language to my own liking and take ultimate responsibility for the content of this publication.

This was done in accordance with the OpenAI API policy and OpenAI's Content Policy or Terms of Use.

# Table of Contents

# Preface

Welcome, fellow tinkerers and code connoisseurs, to this handy guide for all those who've dabbled in the dark arts of software development but haven't quite followed the beaten path of traditional education or careers. Here, we'll embark on a journey into the enchanting world of software commercialization, covering the essentials and sprinkling in some clever principles for turning your digital creations into cold, hard cash.

Picture me, just a wee enthusiast of technology, growing up with a burning passion for building, coding, and unraveling the mysteries of the digital realm. When I finally decided to take the plunge and turn my hobby into something more, I found myself swimming in a sea of uncertainty. I loved designing, developing, and sharing my creations, but the thought of a 9-to-5 grind learning the ropes of selling and distributing software was, frankly, unappetizing.

As it turns out, there are others like me who've enjoyed this path as a hobby without ever making it their life's work. If you're one of these spirited souls, or if you're just dipping your toes into the coding pool, this book is for you. After all, you could be the mastermind behind the next game-changer or revolution, and you shouldn't let the unknown hinder your progress.

So, if you're brimming with ideas and ready to take on the world, but feeling a tad overwhelmed by the prospect of turning your digital dreams into reality, fear not! This book has got you covered. Spoiler alert: it's easier than you think.

I'm beyond excited to see what ingenious inventions you'll bring to life, how you'll shake up your own existence, and which norms or industries you'll leave quaking in your wake.

*Tommy Burke*

# Chapter 1.
# An Introduction to Software Commercialization

Alright, fellow code-wranglers, let's talk about turning your software development passion into a steady flow of cash. I know, I know, we love building things for the joy of it. But hey, a little extra dough never hurt anybody, right? In this book, we'll be exploring the exciting world of software commercialization, where code meets commerce.

Now, before we get too deep into things, let me clear up some semantics. You might think this book is all about proprietary software, but hold your horses! We're all about commercializing your hard work, whether it's open-source or closed-source. So, let's dive in and start making sense of it all.

## THE COMMERCIAL VS. PROPRIETARY SHOWDOWN

When we talk about commercializing software, we're referring to the noble art of monetizing and selling your digital creations. This is in line with the GNU philosophy, which states that commercial doesn't have to mean proprietary. That's right, you can have your cake and eat it too!

As you read on, remember that there are plenty of ways to commercialize your work. Choosing between open-source and proprietary is like picking your favorite pizza topping: entirely up to you and your appetite.

## COMMERCIALIZING CLOSED SOURCE: THE SECRET SAUCE

Closed-source or proprietary software is like that secret family recipe you don't want to share with anyone. You develop software, protect your intellectual property (IP), and distribute it to the world in binary form, with licenses to keep sneaky hands off your code.

This model lets you protect your IP and set up shop like a traditional business, creating and selling products without worrying about someone stealing or duplicating your hard-earned code. It's a classic approach, tried and true. But, as with any good story, there's more than one path to follow.

## COMMERCIALIZING OPEN SOURCE: SHARING IS CARING (& PROFITABLE)

We'll get into the nitty-gritty of open-source commercialization in Chapter 2, but let's start by busting a myth: open-source does not mean you can't monetize your software. In fact, the GNU philosophy encourages it! It's even necessary sometimes for the survival of free software.

Just be cautious about license terms when working with existing open-source platforms. You wouldn't want to accidentally break any rules and ruin the party, would you?

For more info on the GNU philosophy and how to be a good open-source citizen, check out their documentation at: https://www.gnu.org/philosophy/philosophy.html

Now that we've laid the groundwork, get ready to embark on your journey of software commercialization. Who knows, you might just end up disrupting an industry or two along the way!

# Chapter 2.
# Open-Source and Commercial Licensing

In this chapter, we'll embark on a thrilling journey through the world of open-source and commercial licensing. Buckle up, because we're going to explore common open-source licenses, the nitty-gritty of developing proprietary software from open-source projects, and the art of crafting a software license that'll keep you out of trouble.

Now, you might be wondering why I chose to dive into open-source licensing right at the beginning. Well, it's a bit like choosing which sock to put on first in the morning – there's no definitive right answer, but it does feel like an essential topic to tackle early on when creating proprietary or commercial software.

Using open-source software as a foundation for your own proprietary masterpiece can be a real time and resource saver. Plus, you get to tap into an existing community of passionate developers. But beware, young padawan, because with great code comes great responsibility. You'll need to know the legal and practical considerations of open-source software, like licensing requirements and potential liability.

Open-source software is like a gift from the coding gods, with licenses that grant us mere mortals the freedom to use, modify, and distribute their sacred creations. But turning that gift into a profitable business isn't always a walk in the park. You'll need to examine the fine print of open-source licenses and decipher the obligations or restrictions they impose.

Fear not, for we shall cover a variety of open-source licenses in this chapter, giving you the knowledge to pick the best one for your project. Some licenses, like the GNU General Public License (GPL), are the gatekeepers of open-source code, ensuring it remains freely available for others to modify and distribute. These "copyleft" licenses come with strings attached; any software built using the open-source code must abide by the same terms.

On the other hand, some licenses, like the suave and debonair MIT License or the sophisticated Apache License, are more permissive. They let you use and modify open-source code without forcing you to share your precious source code with the world. In other words, you can build proprietary software and sell access to it without feeling obliged to offer your code on a silver platter.

So, let's dive into the marvelous world of open-source and commercial licensing, and together we'll uncover the secrets, pitfalls, and opportunities that await.

## COMMERCIALIZING OPEN-SOURCE

Ready to dive into the fascinating world of commercializing open-source software? Great! Let's unravel the mysteries of turning your open-source project into a money-making machine while exploring the two main approaches to commercial software development.

Commercial software is the digital equivalent of a secret family recipe, usually sold to users and guarded by intellectual property laws like copyrights and patents. Developers often turn to open-source software as a starting point or ingredient in their proprietary concoctions.

Now, let's talk about the two approaches you can take when developing and distributing commercial software: keeping the source code under wraps or releasing it to the masses.

First up, we have the hush-hush method where the source code remains a secret, known only to the development team. This popular approach lets software companies maintain control over their software's inner workings and stand out from the crowd. However, it does come with a downside: others can't access or modify the source code, which might limit customization or integration with other systems.

The alternative is to release the source code under an open-source license, letting anyone access and modify your digital masterpiece. This can lead to widespread adoption and even community contributions to your project. But beware, as you won't be able to stop others from using, distributing, or even selling your software, which might impact your bottom line.

Don't worry, though – you can still make money with this second approach, known as "open-source commercial software." Even with the source code out in the open, you can sell the software as a standalone product or part of a larger solution. You can also monetize through services like support, training, and customization. And let's not forget the community contributions and improvements, which can make your software even more valuable over time.

So, the million-dollar question is: are you willing to release your source code? There are valid arguments for both sides, but your choice will significantly influence your options. If the open-source project has a permissive license allowing commercial use, you can build your commercial software on its foundation. However, if it has a copyleft license, you might need to release your commercial software's source code as well.

Once you've gone through the list of licenses at the end of this chapter, don't forget to consider including attributions or other notices required by the open-source license in your commercial software. Also, think about the implications of using open-source software on your own intellectual property and whether you need a separate license or other measures to protect your rights.

With all this newfound knowledge, you'll be well-prepared to make an informed decision and turn your open-source passion project into a profitable venture.

## PERMISSIVE VS. NON-PERMISSIVE

Alright, let's dive into the world of permissive versus non-permissive licensing and how copyleft software fits into the equation when creating commercialized software platforms.

In the realm of permissive licensed open-source platforms, you're pretty much free to use the open-source code as you please, without the need to release your own source code or credit the original developers. This freedom means you can monetize and sell the platform commercially without any strings attached.

But beware, my fellow developer, as non-permissive licensed open-source platforms come with their own set of terms and conditions. When using this type of open-source code, you might need to release your source code, credit the original developers, or even distribute your platform under the same open-source license. Fear not, though – you can still monetize and sell your platform commercially, as long as you abide by the terms of the non-permissive open-source license.

## COPYLEFT SOFTWARE

Now, let's talk about copyleft software. When you use an open-source platform with a non-permissive license to create your commercialized software, you must comply with the license's terms. In many cases, this means your commercial software's source code must be made available to users, and you can't keep it secret. But worry not, because you can still sell the software and charge a fee, as long as you follow the non-permissive license's terms.

Imagine you create a software platform incorporating or based on software licensed under the GNU GPL. In this case, you must release your entire platform under the GNU GPL, which requires you to make the source code available to users and license your entire program under the same terms. This means others can use, modify, and distribute your software platform under the GNU GPL, but you can still charge a fee and monetize it through distribution and support services.

With the GNU GPL, you're free to charge for your software and monetize it through distribution and support services. However, you can't stop others from doing the same, as the GNU GPL allows users to freely distribute copies of your software (even sell them) if they also provide the source code and license the software under the GNU GPL. This is the infamous "copyleft" provision of the GNU GPL, which ensures that any modified versions of the software are also licensed under the GNU GPL and distributed with the source code.

Understanding these licensing differences is essential when commercializing open-source software, so be sure to have a good understanding of them when making your choice.

## COMPLETELY PROPRIETARY LICENSING

Ah, the world of completely proprietary licensing – the polar opposite of our open-source friends. If you prefer to have exclusive control over selling and monetizing your software, this might be the route for you.

When you release your software under a proprietary license, you call the shots. You have the exclusive right to sell and monetize your software as you see fit, and no one else can do so without your permission. However, this exclusivity comes with a trade-off: your software's source code won't be available to the public, and users won't be able to modify or distribute the software without your say-so.

Now, if you're not quite ready to go full-on proprietary, there are other open-source licenses that allow you to distribute your software commercially while still requiring the source code to be available. Users can modify and distribute the software under certain conditions, and these licenses – like the Mozilla Public License – are the "copyleft" licenses.

So, whether you want to hold your cards close to your chest with a proprietary license or venture into the world of copyleft licensing, the choice is yours. Choose wisely and watch your software thrive in the market!

## DUAL LICENSING

When considering how to license your software, a dual-licensing model can offer the best of both worlds. This approach involves releasing your software under two different licenses, one for free personal use and another for commercial use at a fee. Users can then choose the license that best suits their needs. Dual licensing can take various forms, depending on your goals and objectives as a developer.

For instance, you might offer an open-source license for personal use and a proprietary license for commercial use. This strategy allows you to:

❖ Provide the software freely for personal use while monetizing it for commercial purposes.

❖ Enable users to modify and improve the software for personal use while retaining control over its commercial use.

❖ Foster a community of users around the software, as making it freely available for personal use can encourage more people to use and contribute to its development.

Alternatively, you might release a single software product under a proprietary license that also includes provisions for using open-source components. In this scenario, your software would be closed source and monetized through sales or subscriptions, but the proprietary license would allow users to utilize open-source components while complying with their licenses. This approach can be beneficial if:

❖ You want to protect your software's proprietary features and functionality while still allowing users to access and modify the source code.

❖ You aim to make it easy for users to customize and integrate the software into their systems while still retaining control and protecting your intellectual property.

❖ You want to build a community of users and developers around the software, as making the source code available can encourage more people to use and contribute to its development.

Dual licensing can be a versatile approach to software licensing that accommodates both personal and commercial uses. The specific goals and objectives of a developer will depend on the nature of the software and its intended use. As always, it is essential to carefully consider the terms of the license and the software's intended use when choosing a dual-licensing model.

## COMMON OPEN-SOURCE LICENSES

There are various open-source licenses available, each with different terms and requirements. A few examples include:

❖ **MIT License**: A permissive license with minimal restrictions, requiring only that users include a copy of the license and copyright notice in the software.

❖ **Apache License**: A permissive license that requires users to include a copy of the license and a disclaimer of warranty in the software.

❖ **GNU General Public License (GPL)**: A copyleft license that mandates users distribute the software under the same license and provide access to the source code.

- ❖ **GNU Lesser General Public License (LGPL)**: A less restrictive copyleft license that allows users to incorporate the software into proprietary software without releasing the source code.

- ❖ **Mozilla Public License**: A permissive license requiring users to include a copy of the license and notice of any changes made to the software.

- ❖ **BSD License**: A permissive license that requires users to include a copy of the license and notice of copyright in the software.

- ❖ **Creative Commons License**: A set of licenses offering various usage, modification, and distribution rights depending on the specific terms of the license. Often used for non-software works like music, art, and text.

- ❖ **Eclipse Public License**: A permissive license requiring users to include a copy of the license and notice of any changes made to the software.

- ❖ **Artistic License**: A permissive license that requires users to include a copy of the license and notice of any changes made to the software.

- ❖ **GNU Affero General Public License (AGPL)**: A copyleft license similar to the GPL, designed specifically for software used over a network, requiring users to make the source code available to users who interact with the software over a network.

Always read and understand the full terms of any license before using it as the basis for your software project.

## ADDITIONAL OPEN-SOURCE CONSIDERATIONS

When building on or incorporating open-source software into your own projects, there may be other factors to consider, depending on your business and goals. These may include:

Reputation: Evaluate the reputation of the open-source project to ensure it aligns with your goals and quality standards.

Community support: Consider the level of community support and involvement, as this can impact the project's development and your ability to get help when needed.

Long-term viability: Assess the project's long-term viability to ensure it will remain active and supported in the future.

Carefully consider these factors when deciding whether and how to incorporate open-source software into your own projects. This will help ensure the success and sustainability of your software in the long run.

# Chapter 3.
# Developing Your Application

Ahoy, code-slingers! Welcome to the third chapter of our adventurous voyage, "Developing Your Application." While we're not here to hold your hand through the entire process (we trust you're already skilled in that department), we will remind you of some important concepts and considerations that may have slipped your mind. After all, no one wants their digital baby to flop because they overlooked something crucial.

In this chapter, we'll steer you through the murky waters of software development by touching on seven key areas:

1. The Fundamentals of Software Development

2. Software Development Methodologies

3. Portability

4. Testing

5. Security

6. Project Management

7. Documentation

As we navigate these topics, we'll shed light on various development methodologies (think agile, waterfall, and lean) and help you pick the perfect approach for your unique project. We'll also discuss the significance of portability, so your brainchild can thrive across different devices and operating systems.

Next, we'll dive into testing (because no one wants a buggy app) and security, because a vulnerable application is a hacker's dream come true. And finally, we'll touch on project management and documentation, those oft-overlooked but oh-so-important aspects that can make or break your software's commercial success.

By the end of this chapter, you'll have refreshed your memory on the vital principles of software development and be ready to set sail on your journey to build and distribute your very own commercial software. So, anchors aweigh, and let's get cracking!

## THE FUNDAMENTALS OF SOFTWARE DEVELOPMENT

Behold, the mighty pillars of software development! These core principles, concepts, and skills are the lifeblood of every digital masterpiece. Let's take a whirlwind tour through some of the fundamentals that every programmer worth their salt should know:

❖ **Programming Languages**: Be it C++, Java, Python, or C#, knowing at least one programming language is as essential as a painter knowing their colors.

❖ **Data Structures & Algorithms**: Master the art of organizing data with arrays, linked lists, and trees, and wield algorithms to solve problems like a coding ninja.

❖ **Object-Oriented Programming (OOP)**: Ah, the classic paradigm of objects representing real-world entities. Embrace OOP for modular and reusable problem-solving.

❖ **Software Design Patterns**: These reusable solutions to common design woes are like secret weapons in your programming arsenal.

❖ **Testing & Debugging**: Keep your software spick-and-span with test cases, debugging tools, and techniques like unit testing and continuous integration.

❖ **Version Control**: Git your act together and learn how to manage your codebase's evolution like a pro.

- ❖ **Collaboration & Communication**: Teamwork makes the dream work! Hone your communication skills and get comfy with project management tools.

- ❖ **Problem-Solving**: Flex those brain muscles and learn how to break down complex problems into bite-sized chunks.

- ❖ **Documentation**: It may not be glamorous, but clear documentation is essential for keeping your project shipshape over time.

- ❖ **Professionalism**: Stand tall and follow best practices, meet deadlines, and adhere to ethical principles.

- ❖ **Lifecycle Management**: Master the software development lifecycle (SDLC) stages for smooth sailing from concept to completion.

- ❖ **Security**: Don your digital armor and protect your application with security best practices.

- ❖ **Scalability**: Design your software to grow and evolve gracefully, like a well-tended garden.

- ❖ **Performance**: Ensure your application is as responsive as a caffeinated squirrel, optimizing for the best user experience.

- ❖ **Maintainability**: Build software that can adapt and endure, like a trusty Swiss Army knife.

- ❖ **Deployment:** Learn to navigate the treacherous waters of deployment, from configuring infrastructure to launching in the target environment.

- ❖ **Continuous Integration & Delivery**: Embrace CI/CD to automate the build, test, and deployment process like a well-oiled machine.

- ❖ **DevOps**: Bridge the gap between development and operations, fostering collaboration and communication for faster, more reliable software delivery.

❖ **Cloud Computing**: Unleash the power of the cloud to build and deploy applications more efficiently and cost-effectively.

❖ **Artificial Intelligence & Machine Learning**: Stay on the cutting edge by incorporating AI and ML technologies into your software creations.

And there you have it, a crash course in the fundamentals of software development! Keep these in mind as you set off on your journey to build and distribute your own commercial software.

## SOFTWARE DEVELOPMENT METHODOLOGIES

Choosing the right software development methodology is like picking the perfect dance partner: it's all about the rhythm, style, and coordination. Let's take a quick look at three popular methodologies: Agile, Waterfall, and Lean.

Imagine Agile as freestyle dancing. It's flexible, collaborative, and adapts to the beat. Agile incorporates "sprints" to keep development cycles short and snappy, making it perfect for projects where the direction may be uncertain. Agile is like software yoga - highly flexible and responsive to change. Its rapid iteration and delivery keep your groove going, while collaboration and communication harmoniously create beautiful music. However, Agile might not be the best fit for projects that are set in stone, and it can be challenging if the team isn't committed to the Agile mindset.

Now, picture Waterfall as a classical ballroom dance. It follows a linear, sequential approach that leaves no room for improvisation. Waterfall is great for projects where the steps are well-defined, and the tempo is steady. It provides a clear and structured approach, much like a well-choreographed routine. But it's not the best choice when you need to change tempo or direction, and it doesn't allow for rapid iteration and delivery—think waltz, not salsa.

Lean, on the other hand, is the breakdancer of methodologies. It's efficient, focused, and always seeking improvement. Lean is all about rapid prototyping, iteration, and maximizing value for your audience. It emphasizes continuous improvement, akin to a dancer always perfecting their moves. However, Lean might not be the best fit for projects with well-defined requirements and a high level of certainty. Moreover, it can be tough to implement if the team isn't fully committed to the Lean lifestyle.

Remember, the right methodology for your project depends on your specific goals and needs. Take the time to weigh the strengths and limitations of each before you decide which dance partner to twirl around the software development dance floor with!

## PORTABILITY

Portability is like a passport for your software, allowing it to travel across different devices, operating systems, or environments with ease. Ensuring your software is portable can expand your market and make it more user-friendly.

To develop portable software, imagine you're preparing for an international trip. First, choose a well-traveled programming language, like Python or Java, which is familiar with different platforms and makes it easier for users to run your software wherever they go. Next, pack cross-platform libraries and frameworks, such as Qt or GTK, that work well on different platforms, reducing the need for platform-specific code.

As you travel, always dress for the destination. Keep your target platform in mind while designing your software, making sure it looks good in different screen resolutions and window sizes. Before embarking on your journey, test-drive different platforms to ensure your software works well, identifying any issues and guaranteeing a smooth user experience.

For some bonus travel tips, consider sticking to portable file formats like PDF or CSV, avoiding platform-specific tourist traps, embracing local cultures by localizing your software, and traveling light with portable hardware. By following these tips, your software's portability will soar, making it more accessible, user-friendly, and increasing its market potential.

## TESTING

Testing is like a software's personal trainer, keeping it in tip-top shape and ready to meet the needs of its users. From unit testing to integration and acceptance testing, there are plenty of ways to put your software through its paces.

When giving your software a good workout, think of it as embarking on a fitness journey. Start by testing early and often, just like any exercise routine. This helps to spot any issues quickly, saving time and effort later on. Next, automate your testing regime using tools and frameworks, making the process less labor-intensive while improving test reliability and coverage.

Mix up your testing techniques by employing a variety of exercises, such as unit, integration, and acceptance testing, to ensure your software is in peak condition. Test on different platforms to identify any platform-specific quirks and flex those edge cases by testing for unusual scenarios.

Now, let's dive deeper into the different testing exercises. Unit testing is like focusing on individual muscles, integration testing checks if your software's components are team players, and acceptance testing evaluates your software from the user's perspective.

But, if you want to maximize your gains and keep your software in top shape, remember to use extra testing techniques like regression testing, performance testing, and security testing. By using a variety of testing exercises, you'll be giving your software a comprehensive workout, ensuring it functions correctly and meets user expectations.

❖ Regression Testing: After making changes to your software, re-test it to ensure no new issues have cropped up. It's like making sure an old injury doesn't flare up again.

❖ Performance Testing: Test your software's stamina, such as response time, throughput, or resource usage, to identify any potential performance issues.

❖ Security Testing: Put your software through cybersecurity boot camp, identifying and addressing vulnerabilities to make sure it's tough enough to withstand attacks.

## SECURITY

Security is the software world's top bodyguard, keeping your users' privacy and data safe from the dangers of the digital realm. From encryption to authentication and access controls, there's a whole arsenal of tools to protect your software's VIPs.

Next up, are some guidelines for making your software's security entourage the best it can be. By following these guidelines, you'll create a top-notch security detail for your software, earning the trust and confidence of your users and ensuring your software's integrity.

❖ **Encrypt Data**: Like a secret code, encryption keeps sensitive data such as passwords and financial information safe from prying eyes.

❖ **Implement Authentication**: Set up a bouncer in the form of login credentials to ensure only authorized users get access to the party.

❖ **Control Access**: Put different users on different guest lists, limiting the data and functionality they can access to keep things exclusive.

❖ **Regularly Test & Update**: Stay ahead of security threats by frequently testing and updating your software like an ever-evolving security playbook.

❖ **Use Secure Communication Channels**: Go undercover by using secure channels like HTTPS or SSL when transmitting data between your software and external systems.

❖ **Store Data Securely**: Keep your users' data in a digital vault with encrypted databases or file systems.

❖ **Practice Secure Coding**: Follow secure coding practices, such as input validation and error handling, to make your software as tough as nails against vulnerabilities.

❖ **Educate Your Users**: Turn your users into security-savvy sidekicks by teaching them the importance of security and how to protect their data.

## PROJECT MANAGEMENT

As you embark on your software development journey, it's essential to master the art of project management. In the upcoming narrative, you'll be guided through the steps for managing a software development project like a rock star. With this approach, you'll not only learn the key tasks but also learn how to orchestrate a successful project that hits all the right notes!

Once upon a time in the realm of software development, there was a project manager on a quest to orchestrate a successful project. The journey began with *DEFINING THE SCOPE AND OBJECTIVES*, setting the stage with a clear vision of the project's deliverables and measurable goals.

To bring the project to life, our hero crafted a master plan, composing the ultimate setlist of tasks, dependencies, and resources needed to complete the project. The next step was *ASSEMBLING A TALENTED LINEUP OF PROS* with the skills and expertise to rock the project.

With the band together, they *IDENTIFIED AND MANAGED RISKS* that might throw them off course, always ready to adapt and adjust to keep the show going. They embraced the fast-paced tempo of *AGILE METHODOLOGIES*, like Scrum, to ensure rapid iteration and continuous delivery.

Throughout the journey, our project manager vigilantly *MONITORED PROGRESS AND TRACKED RESULTS*, using powerful tools like Asana, Trello, or Jira to keep everything in tune. *COMMUNICATION WAS KEY*; they regularly updated their fans (stakeholders) on the project's progress and addressed any concerns that arose.

*REALISTIC TIMELINES* and *CAREFUL MANAGEMENT OF DEPENDENCIES* between tasks ensured the project didn't miss a beat. By *SETTING CLEAR GOALS AND EXPECTATIONS*, everyone in the band and the audience (team and stakeholders) knew what a successful performance looked like.

And finally, our project manager *KEPT THE BAND MEMBERS FIRED UP* by providing support, resources, and celebrating their solos (contributions) in the project.

## DOCUMENTATION

In the software development world, documentation is like the script to a blockbuster movie – it sets the stage for users to navigate the software with ease and confidence. A well-documented software not only enhances the user experience but also simplifies maintenance and future development. Let's dive into the types of documentation you'll need and how to make them shine.

Imagine you're the proud creator of an innovative software, and it's time to write the user manual. This is where you explain the software's features and capabilities, guiding users through common tasks. Think of it as a friendly tour guide, helping users navigate the software with ease.

Next on the list is API documentation. If the user manual is a tour guide, API documentation is the software's encyclopedia. This reference manual provides detailed information about the software's application programming interface (API), including the functions, classes, and methods it offers. Don't forget to include examples – they're the icing on the cake, showing users how to make the most of the API.

Last but not least, technical specifications are like the blueprints of a building, detailing the software's technical aspects, such as hardware and software requirements, architecture, and design. These documents help other developers and stakeholders grasp the inner workings of the software.

Now, let's make sure your documentation stands out from the crowd:

1. **Embrace Clarity & Conciseness**: Write with simplicity and precision, avoiding technical jargon and complex concepts that may confuse users.

2. **Show, Don't Just Tell**: Use examples and illustrations to demonstrate concepts and provide context, making the documentation more engaging and accessible.

3. **Organize with Purpose**: Arrange the documentation logically and use headings, subheadings, and a table of contents or index to help users find what they need quickly.

4. **Stay Up-to-Date**: Keep the documentation current as the software evolves, ensuring its relevance and accuracy.

With well-crafted, clear, and comprehensive documentation, you'll pave the way for users to enjoy your software to its fullest potential, boosting adoption and usage while creating a positive user experience.

# Chapter 4.
# Packaging Your Application

Ah, the sweet smell of a freshly built application, just waiting to be released into the wild. It's an exhilarating moment, isn't it? But before you start popping the champagne and toasting to your success, there's still some work left to do. Development was just the opening act; now it's time for the main event.

In this chapter, we'll dive into the nitty-gritty of preparing your software for distribution. We'll explore the glamorous world of software licenses, delve into the thrilling realm of package management systems, and even learn how to create installation and uninstallation packages that your users will adore. And to top it off, we'll discuss the secretive art of code obfuscation. By the end of this chapter, you'll be a veritable packaging master, ready to unleash your creation upon the masses.

To package and sell your application, you'll need to jump through a few hoops to make sure everything is shipshape and meets any pesky legal requirements. Here are some steps to guide you on your journey:

1. **Test, Test, Test**: Make sure your application is stable and functional by testing it on various systems and configurations. If you're feeling a bit rusty on testing, feel free to revisit the "testing" section in the previous chapter.

2. **Pick a License**: Select a software license that suits your needs and protects your interests. We'll dive into proprietary and dual licensing shortly, but if you're leaning towards an open-source license, check out "Common Open-Source Licenses" in chapter 1.

3. **Create Installation and Uninstallation Packages**: Craft an installer that makes it a breeze for users to set up your software, and an uninstaller for when they're ready to part ways. We'll cover this in

detail later in the chapter, along with what to include in your software bundle.

4. **Document, Document, Document**: Ensure you have user guides, installation instructions, and any other documentation that will help users navigate your masterpiece. If you need a refresher on documentation, take a peek at the previous chapter.

5. **Set Up a Storefront**: Create a website or use an online store platform to sell your application. You'll need marketing materials, pricing info, and a system for processing payments and delivering your software. But don't worry, we'll tackle these topics in a later chapter, "Distribution and Delivery."

6. **Promote Like a Pro**: Spread the word about your application through various channels, such as social media, online forums, or advertising. We'll cover this in another exciting chapter, "Marketing and Promotion."

Keep in mind that selling your application commercially can be a complex process, requiring a significant investment of time and resources. If you're feeling out of your depth, don't hesitate to seek the assistance of a seasoned professional or an experienced mentor to help you navigate these treacherous waters.

## SOFTWARE LICENSES

In this section, we'll delve into the thrilling world of proprietary software licenses. But before we dive into the deep end, let's clear up a few potential misunderstandings, namely the differences between software licenses, software license agreements, and our dear friends, the End User License Agreements (EULAs). Buckle up; it's about to get interesting!

## SOFTWARE LICENSES VS. SLAS VS. EULAS

A proprietary software license is like a secret handshake between you and the users of your software. It's a legal document that sets the ground rules for using and distributing your software, granting rights and privileges while safeguarding your intellectual property, managing risk, and making sure everyone is singing from the same hymn sheet.

On the other hand, a proprietary software licensing agreement (which we'll cover later in "Intellectual Property") is more of a catch-all term. It refers to the grander process of licensing your intellectual property (IP) to others in exchange for payment or other considerations. These agreements can encompass various types of IP, from software and trademarks to patents and copyrighted works.

To sum it up, a proprietary software license is a specific legal document relating to the use and distribution of software, while a proprietary software licensing agreement is a broader term, encompassing the licensing of various types of IP.

Now, let's talk about software licenses and EULAs. A software license is a legal agreement between you—the developer or distributor of a software product—and the user, outlining the terms and conditions for using your software. It grants certain rights but also specifies restrictions on how the software can be used.

An End User License Agreement (EULA), on the other hand, is a specific type of software license presented as a document that the user must accept before installing or using your software. Like a software license, a EULA sets forth the terms and conditions for using your software, but it's a legally binding agreement between you and the end user.

Developers and distributors might use a software license, a EULA, or both to govern their software products. The choice between the two depends on your goals and objectives, the nature of your software, and your target audience. Generally, EULAs are more suited to consumer-facing software, while software licenses are better for software distributed to businesses or organizations.

Now that we've cleared that up, let's get back to the main event: software licenses. Picking the right software license is a crucial step in creating and selling proprietary software. It's a legal agreement that outlines how your software can be used, distributed, and modified. With a smorgasbord of licenses to choose from, each with its own terms and conditions, it's essential to select the one that aligns with your business goals and your software's intended use.

As we've already covered various other licenses in chapter 1, here, we'll focus solely on the fascinating world of proprietary licensing.

## PROPRIETARY SOFTWARE LICENSES

And now, ladies and gentlemen, we present a marvelous example of a proprietary software license, just for you!

**Software License**

This Software License (the "License") is a legal agreement between [Name of Licensor] (the "Licensor") and [Name of Licensee] (the "Licensee") for the use of the software [Name of Software] (the "Software").

**1. Grant of License.** The Licensor grants to the Licensee a non-exclusive, non-transferable, limited license to use the Software for the following purposes: [Purposes of use, such as personal use, commercial use, educational use, etc.].

**2. Restrictions.** The Licensee shall not:
　(a) Modify, adapt, or translate the Software.
　(b) Reverse engineer, decompile, or disassemble the Software.
　(c) Sell, rent, lease, or sublicense the Software.
　(d) Remove any proprietary notices or labels on the Software.

**3. Intellectual Property Rights.** The Licensor retains all right, title, and interest in and to the Software, including all intellectual property rights. The Licensee shall not claim any ownership rights in the Software.

**4. Termination.** The License shall terminate automatically if the Licensee breaches any of the terms and conditions of the License. Upon termination, the Licensee shall cease all use of the Software and destroy all copies of the Software.

**5. Disclaimer of Warranty.** The Software is provided "as is" without warranty of any kind, either express or implied, including, but not limited to, the implied warranties of merchantability, fitness for a particular purpose, or non-infringement.

**6. Limitation of Liability.** In no event shall the Licensor be liable for any damages, including, but not limited to, direct, indirect, special, incidental, or consequential damages, arising out of the use or inability to use the Software, even if the Licensor has been advised of the possibility of such damages.

**7. Governing Law.** This License shall be governed by and construed in accordance with the laws of the [State/Country].

---

**Software License (continued)**

**8. Entire Agreement.** This License constitutes the entire agreement between the Licensor and the Licensee and supersedes all prior or contemporaneous understandings or agreements, whether oral or written.

**9. Waiver.** The failure of the Licensor to exercise or enforce any right or provision of this License shall not constitute a waiver of such right or provision.

**10. Severability.** If any provision of this License is found to be invalid or unenforceable, that provision shall be enforced to the maximum extent possible, and the remaining provisions shall remain in full force and effect.

IN WITNESS WHEREOF, the parties have executed this License as of the date and year first above written.

[Name of Licensor] [Name of Licensee]

---

When crafting your very own proprietary software license, consider the following tips, brought to you by experts in the field:

❖ **Choose the Right Licensing Model**: With a buffet of options like proprietary, open-source, or hybrid, the perfect licensing model awaits you. Just remember, each has its pros and cons, so choose wisely based on your business goals and objectives.

❖ **Define the Scope of the License**: The scope encompasses the rights and privileges granted to your esteemed licensees. Be crystal clear about the purposes of use, restrictions, and duration of the license in your agreement.

❖ **Protect your Intellectual Property Rights**: Don your superhero cape, and ensure your intellectual property rights are protected in the agreement. Prohibit licensees from modifying, adapting, or reverse engineering your software, and demand respect for your ownership rights.

❖ **Include Disclaimers & Limitations of Liability**: To limit your liability and risk, incorporate disclaimers and limitations in the agreement.

Include provisions that disclaim warranties, limit damages, and exclude certain types of damages.

With a clearly defined proprietary software license outlining the terms and conditions for distribution and use, you'll safeguard your intellectual property rights, manage risk, and ensure that you and your licensees harmoniously coexist.

## PROPRIETARY DUAL-LICENSED SOFTWARE LICENSES

Should your product spring forth from an existing open-source project, don't forget to account for and communicate that in your software license, in line with the open-source license's terms.

Behold, a sample template for a proprietary software license, perfect for products with proprietary features, code, and capabilities built on top of an existing open-source project:

---

**Proprietary Software License**

This Proprietary Software License (the "License") is a legal agreement between [Name of Licensor] ("Licensor") and you ("Licensee") for the [Name of Software] software (the "Software"). By downloading, installing, or using the Software, you accept the terms and conditions of this License. If you do not agree to the terms and conditions of this License, do not download, install, or use the Software.

---

**Proprietary Software License (continued)**

**1. Grant of License.** Licensor grants to Licensee a limited, non-exclusive, non-transferable, and revocable license to use the Software for the following purposes:

[Purpose of License, e.g., personal use, commercial use, educational use]

**2. Ownership.** The Software is owned by Licensor and is protected by copyright laws and international treaty provisions. Licensee acknowledges that the Software contains proprietary features, code, and capabilities that are not part of the underlying open-source project. Licensee agrees not to modify, translate, reverse engineer, decompile, disassemble, or create derivative works of the Software, except as permitted by law.

**3. Open-Source License.** The Software is based on an existing open-source project and is subject to the terms and conditions of the [Name of Open-Source License] open-source license (the "Open-Source License"). Licensee agrees to comply with the terms and conditions of the Open-Source License, including any requirements to make the source code of the Software available to the public.

**4. Term and Termination.** This License is effective until terminated. Licensee may terminate this License at any time by destroying all copies of the Software. This License will also terminate if Licensee fails to comply with any term or condition of this License. Upon termination, Licensee must destroy all copies of the Software.

**5. Disclaimer of Warranty.** The Software is provided "as is" and without any warranty of any kind. Licensor does not warrant that the Software will meet the requirements or expectations of Licensee, or that the operation of the Software will be uninterrupted or error-free.

**6. Limitation of Liability.** Licensor shall not be liable for any damages arising out of the use or inability to use the Software, including but not limited to direct, indirect, incidental, consequential, or punitive damages.

**7. Governing Law.** This License shall be governed by and construed in accordance with the laws of [Name of Jurisdiction].

---

**Proprietary Software License (continued)**

**8. Entire Agreement.** This License constitutes the entire agreement between Licensor and Licensee, and supersedes all prior or contemporaneous agreements or understandings, whether oral or written. This License may not be amended or modified except in writing signed by both parties.

**9. Waiver.** The failure of the Licensor to exercise or enforce any right or provision of this License shall not constitute a waiver of such right or provision.

**10. Severability.** If any provision of this License is found to be invalid or unenforceable, that provision shall be enforced to the maximum extent possible, and the remaining provisions shall remain in full force and effect.

IN WITNESS WHEREOF, the parties have executed this License as of the date and year first above written.

[Name of Licensor] [Name of Licensee]

---

This magnificent template serves as a foundation for a proprietary software license suited for products featuring proprietary elements built upon an open-source project. It grants users a limited license to use the software for specific purposes, while acknowledging both the proprietary nature of the software and the underlying open-source project. Moreover, it includes provisions for compliance with the open-source project.

This license template artfully protects your software's proprietary aspects while clearly communicating that the open-source components remain, well, open-source. It grants users a limited license to use the software for specific purposes, while acknowledging both the proprietary nature of the software and the underlying open-source project. It also includes provisions for compliance with the open-source license, such as requiring users to make the source code of the software available to the public.

By incorporating these provisions in your license, you'll ensure that the proprietary aspects of your software are well-protected and that users are aware of their obligations regarding the open-source components of the software. In doing so, you'll clearly define users' rights and responsibilities, preventing any misunderstandings or disputes about using your fantastic software.

## PACKAGE MANAGEMENT SYSTEMS

In the awe-inspiring world of software development, package management systems are like the Mary Poppins of tools – practically perfect in every way. They install, update, and manage software packages on a computer, and each has its own set of fabulous features and capabilities. But remember, you must choose one that suits your software and intended user base.

Now, let's dive into an example to see how these magical tools work in practice: PyPI!

### PyPI: THE PYTHON PACKAGE SUPERSTAR

PyPI (Python Package Index) is a package management system for Python, allowing developers to publish and distribute packages to their adoring users. Here's a step-by-step guide to using PyPI:

1. **Create a package**: First, you'll need a setup.py file with all the important metadata (e.g., name, version, dependencies). Don't forget to create a `MANIFEST.in` file that specifies which files to include in the package.

2. **Upload to PyPI**: With the twine tool (a command-line utility), create a package and upload it to the PyPI server.

3. **Users, start your engines**: After you've uploaded your package, users can install your application using the pip tool, simply by running the `pip install` command and specifying your package's name.

4. **Hosting your own package repository**: Want more control? Use a tool like `devpi` to manage packages on your own server.

5. **Distribute packages**: Whether through a simple download link, an online store, or a subscription service, you'll need a way to distribute your packages to users.

6. **Update and maintain**: Keep your packages fresh by uploading new versions and distributing them to users, who can then install updates automatically or manually.

Now, PyPI is great for distributing and managing free and open-source software, as well as commercial and proprietary software. But keep in mind, PyPI is an open-source platform, which means packages published on the platform must be open-source and available under an open-source license. So, it may not be suitable for all commercial and proprietary software.

## OTHER OPTIONS FOR COMMERCIAL & PROPRIETARY SOFTWARE

If PyPI isn't quite right for your commercial and proprietary software, consider using a different package management system or hosting your own package repository. One option is `devpi`, which lets you host your own package repository and gives you more control over distribution and proprietary licenses.

Ultimately, the ideal approach for distributing and managing commercial and proprietary software depends on your specific needs and requirements. Consider your application's complexity, your user base size, and other factors when deciding on the best way to distribute and manage your packages.

## INSTALLATION PACKAGES

Lights, camera, installation packages! These little heroes contain everything needed to install and set up a software application on a computer. When distributing your software, creating an installation package is a must-have, ensuring users can easily install and set up your masterpiece.

## THE MAKING OF AN INSTALLATION PACKAGE: A FIVE-ACT PLAY

1. **Gather Files & Resources**: Assemble all the necessary files and resources needed to install and run the application (e.g., executables, libraries, and configuration files).

2. **Create the Installer**: Using a software tool like InstallShield or WiX, create your installation package. These tools let you specify the files, resources, and installation steps.

3. **Test, Test, Test**: Check that your installer works correctly on different systems.

4. **Create Installation Media**: Whether it's a DVD or a downloadable file, make sure you have the installation media to distribute your package.

5. **Document the Process**: Write up some instructions on how to install and configure the application.

## ONE APPLICATION TO RULE THEM ALL: CROSS-OS COMPATIBILITY

To avoid playing favorites with operating systems, consider creating installers for different OSs. Here's how:

❖ **Dedicated Installation Tool**: Use tools like InstallShield, WiX, or Inno Setup to create a multi-OS installer.

❖ **Packaging Tool**: Some development environments, such as Visual Studio, offer packaging tools for creating installers.

❖ **Script it**: For simple applications, consider using a script (e.g., batch file or shell script) to automate installation.

❖ **Containerize**: Package your application and its dependencies into a container (like Docker) for easy deployment on different operating systems.

## EXTRA CONSIDERATIONS FOR MULTI-OS INSTALLERS

Here are some tips for creating a user-friendly installer that works well on different operating systems:

❖ **Compatibility**: Ensure your installer is compatible with target OSs. Some tools, like InstallShield and WiX, allow multi-OS compatibility.

❖ **Prerequisites**: Include any required libraries or frameworks in the installer.

❖ **System Requirements**: Make sure the installer checks for system requirements before installation.

❖ **Customization Options**: Offer options like choosing the installation directory or creating a desktop shortcut.

❖ **Uninstallation**: Don't forget an uninstallation feature, so users can remove the application if needed.

Follow these guidelines, and you'll create a stellar installer for your software application that users across different operating systems can appreciate.

## UNINSTALLATION PACKAGES

Now let's talk break-ups – software break-ups, that is! An uninstallation package contains the code and resources needed to remove a software application from a computer. Providing an uninstallation package for your software keeps things friendly and easy for users who no longer want your application.

## THREE UNINSTALLER IDEAS FOR PYTHON APPLICATIONS

❖ **Include an Uninstaller**: Bundle your application with an uninstaller, either as a separate script or executable, that users can run to remove your application.

❖ **Use a Package Management System**: If you're distributing your application through a package management system like PyPI, it may already include an uninstall feature for users.

❖ **Provide Manual Uninstallation Instructions**: Give users a step-by-step guide to manually remove the application and any related files from their device.

## HANDLING DEPENDENCIES: A BALANCING ACT

Uninstalling an application can cause some drama if it also removes dependencies that other applications need. To avoid unintended consequences, consider these options for managing dependencies:

1. **Package Management System**: If you're using a package management system like PyPI, it might handle dependencies for you, uninstalling them or keeping them installed based on other applications' needs.

2. **Dependency Management Tool**: Use a tool like pip to manage dependencies, specifying installation and uninstallation details to maintain consistency across systems.

3. **Manual Dependency Uninstallation Instructions**: Provide a list of dependencies installed with the application and instructions for uninstalling each one.

Whatever method you choose, be sure to give users clear instructions for uninstalling the application and dependencies. Consider offering guidance on backing up their data or migrating to another application if needed. After all, break-ups can be tough, but they don't have to be messy!

## CODE OBFUSCATION

Code obfuscation is like camouflaging your source code, making it harder to understand or reverse-engineer. It can protect proprietary algorithms, techniques, or even keep those pesky hackers at bay. With many approaches available, it's important to find your perfect match.

### TOP THREE DISGUISES FOR PYTHON APPLICATIONS

1. **The Code Obfuscator**: Use a code obfuscator like Pyarmor or Pyminifier to transform your code into a jumbled mess that's functional yet challenging to decipher.

2. **Bytecode Compilation**: Turn your Python code into low-level bytecode that's not human-readable. Use Python's compile function and marshal module to create a file that'll keep snoopers at bay.

3. **Python Executable Packager**: Bundle your Python script and dependencies into a single executable file with tools like PyInstaller or py2exe. The result? A self-contained, source-code-free executable.

### A FRIENDLY REMINDER: THERE'S NO PERFECT DISGUISE

While these methods can make your Python application's code more difficult to read and understand, they're not impervious to reverse engineering or decompilation. Just like a master of disguise can be unmasked, determined individuals can still uncover your code's secrets.

So, there you have it – code obfuscation in a nutshell. Remember to stay vigilant and keep adapting your techniques to maintain a secure and secret codebase.

# Chapter 5.
# Application Bundle Accompaniments

Bundle accompaniments – the unsung heroes of software distribution. These are the trusty sidekicks that help your software leap tall buildings in a single bound, or at least make sure it lands in users' hands without any legal snags or mishaps. Let's take a sneak peek at the ensemble cast that keeps your software in tip-top shape:

❖ User Terms Agreements - The rulebook for your software playground.

❖ Privacy Policies - The key to keeping Big Brother at bay.

❖ Cookie Policies - Your application's personal cookie jar.

❖ Technical Support - The superhero hotline for when things go wrong.

❖ Additional Accompaniments - The cherry on top of your application sundae.

So, buckle up and let's dive into the world of application bundle accompaniments, where we'll ensure your software is ready for prime time, and your users can enjoy a seamless and legally compliant experience!

## USER TERMS AGREEMENTS

Welcome to the world of user terms agreements, the playground monitors of your software empire. User terms are like the bouncer at the nightclub of your software, keeping the riff-raff out and making sure everyone behaves. They cover essential topics like how your software should be used, restrictions on use, intellectual property, and any warranties or liabilities you're willing to take on as the developer.

EULAs, the gatekeepers of your digital realm, usually pop up during installation. Users must accept them before they can frolic freely in your digital playground. In the interest of trust and transparency, it's a good idea to include a refund policy and a warranty in your terms of use. This way, users know what to expect, and it'll help build trust in your brand. After all, nobody wants to feel like they're playing a game of "gotcha" with your software.

## PRIVACY POLICIES

Ah, privacy policies – the superhero sworn to protect your deepest, darkest secrets. In today's digital world, it's crucial to have a clear and transparent privacy policy. It tells your users how you collect, use, and share their personal information, and helps keep you on the right side of the law. Think of it as a security blanket, letting your users know you're not the type to gossip about their private data.

Crafting a well-rounded privacy policy is vital for maintaining trust and ensuring that users feel comfortable sharing their data with you. After all, we've all heard the horror stories about data breaches and companies selling user information to the highest bidder.

## COOKIE POLICIES

Next, let's talk about cookie policies. No, not the kind you find in a bakery – we're talking about the ones that keep track of users' data on websites and in software. Like the nosy neighbor who's always keeping an eye on things, having a clear and transparent cookie policy is essential. It helps users understand how their data is being collected and used, while keeping you compliant with relevant laws and regulations.

Cookies may be small and seemingly harmless, but they play a big role in creating a smooth user experience. A well-crafted cookie policy ensures that your users know exactly what kind of crumbs they're leaving behind as they navigate your digital wonderland.

## TECHNICAL SUPPORT

Next stop: technical support, the unsung heroes of the software world, and the cape-wearing sidekicks to your users' digital adventures. These are the folks who swoop in to save the day when users face issues with your software. It's essential to have a plan for providing technical support, as it can make or break the user experience. After all, nobody wants to deal with frustrated customers – or worse, a pitchfork-wielding mob.

Having a robust technical support system in place, whether it's a website, email, phone number, or even a friendly neighborhood AI chatbot, can be the difference between a five-star review and a scathing takedown. Providing prompt and effective support shows that you care about your users, and it helps maintain a positive relationship with them as they traverse your digital domain.

## ADDITIONAL ACCOMPANIMENTS

Like a fine wine paired with the perfect cheese, there might be other accompaniments that enhance your software offering. Think warranty information, licensing agreements, or marketing materials – anything that makes your software shine. Just remember to pick the right pairings for your unique business.

We still need to dive deep into some crucial points for selling your application commercially. But, if you're feeling overwhelmed, don't worry. We're going to cover all of these things too! Just remember, seeking the guidance of a professional or experienced mentor can help you navigate the complexities of selling and marketing your application.

❖ **Packaging it up** *(covered in chapter 4)*: Create an installation package that includes the application, license, dependencies, and other required files. Make sure the format is suitable for your application type (e.g., Windows installer for desktop apps, APK files for Android apps).

❖ **Update, update, update** *(covered in chapter 8)*: Figure out a system for distributing updates to users and ensure they can easily install them. Nobody likes stale software.

❖ **Refund and warranty policies** *(covered in chapter 7)*: Consider creating policies for refunds and repairs to keep users informed about what to expect if they encounter issues.

❖ **Payment processing and delivery** *(covered in chapter 7)*: Set up a payment gateway and a system for delivering your application to users once they've paid for it. You don't want to keep them waiting.

❖ **Get the word out** *(covered in chapter 9)*: Marketing and promotion are vital for success. Identify your target audience, create appealing marketing materials, and brainstorm ways to reach potential customers (social media, online ads, or other channels).

So, let's keep this train moving! But first, we should take a look at some templates for an end user license agreement, a privacy policy, and a cookie policy, which are coming up next. These templates are designed to be comprehensive and protect your company in all regions. Remember to customize them to fit your specific needs and circumstances, and consult a legal professional if you have any questions.

## A Sample End User License Agreement

**END USER LICENSE AGREEMENT**

This End User License Agreement ("EULA") is a legal agreement between you ("you" or "your") and [Company Name] ("we," "us," or "our") for the software product [Software Product], which includes computer software and may include associated media, printed materials, and online or electronic documentation ("Software").

By installing, copying, or otherwise using the Software, you agree to be bound by the terms of this EULA. If you do not agree to the terms of this EULA, do not install or use the Software.

**LICENSE GRANT**

We grant you a non-exclusive, non-transferable, revocable license to use the Software in accordance with this EULA. You are not allowed to sell, rent, lease, or lend the Software to any third party. You are not allowed to distribute or make the Software available to any third party over a network.

**LIMITATIONS**

You are not allowed to modify, translate, reverse engineer, decompile, or disassemble the Software, or create any derivative works based on the Software. You are not allowed to remove or alter any proprietary notices or labels on the Software.

**INTELLECTUAL PROPERTY**

The Software is protected by copyright and other intellectual property laws. We and our licensors own all right, title, and interest in and to the Software, including all associated intellectual property rights.

**DISCLAIMER OF WARRANTY**

The Software is provided "as is," and we make no representations or warranties of any kind, express or implied, with respect to the Software. We do not warrant that the Software will be free from errors or that it will operate without interruption.

## END USER LICENSE AGREEMENT (continued)

### LIMITATION OF LIABILITY

In no event shall we be liable for any damages whatsoever (including, without limitation, damages for loss of business profits, business interruption, loss of business information, or any other pecuniary loss) arising out of the use or inability to use the Software.

### TERMINATION

This EULA is effective until terminated. You may terminate this EULA at any time by destroying the Software and all copies thereof. This EULA will also terminate if you fail to comply with any term or condition of this EULA. Upon termination, you must destroy the Software and all copies thereof.

### GOVERNING LAW

This EULA shall be governed by and construed in accordance with the laws of the [State/Country] without giving effect to any principles of conflicts of law.

### SEVERABILITY

If any provision of this EULA is found to be invalid or unenforceable, that provision shall be enforced to the maximum extent possible, and the remaining provisions shall remain in full force and effect.

### AMENDMENTS

We reserve the right to modify this EULA at any time, and such modification shall be effective upon posting on our website or otherwise distributing the modified EULA to you. You are responsible for reviewing and becoming familiar with any such modifications. Your use of the Software following any such modification constitutes your acceptance of the terms and conditions of the EULA as modified.

This EULA constitutes the entire agreement between you and us with respect to the Software, and supersedes all prior or contemporaneous communications and proposals, whether oral or written, between you and us.

ACKNOWLEDGEMENT

## A SAMPLE PRIVACY POLICY

**PRIVACY POLICY**

This Privacy Policy ("Policy") explains how [Company Name] ("we," "us," or "our") collects, uses, and shares information about you when you use our websites and online services, including mobile applications (collectively, the "Services").

By using the Services, you agree to the collection, use, and sharing of your information as described in this Policy. If you do not agree with our policies and practices, do not use the Services.

We may change our policies and practices from time to time, and we encourage you to review the Policy whenever you access the Services. If we make material changes to the Policy, we will notify you by revising the date at the top of the Policy and, in some cases, by providing you with additional notice (such as adding a statement to our homepage or sending you a notification).

**INFORMATION WE COLLECT**

We collect information about you in the following ways:

1. Information you provide to us: We collect information you provide directly to us, such as when you create an account, participate in a survey, or contact customer support. This information may include your name, email address, phone number, and any other personal or contact information you choose to provide.

2. Information we collect automatically: When you use the Services, we may collect information about your device and your use of the Services. This information may include your IP address, device type, browser type, operating system, device identifiers, and information about your use of the Services, such as the pages you visit and the features you use. We may also collect location information, such as your device's GPS signal or information about nearby Wi-Fi networks or cell towers.

3. Information from third parties: We may receive information about you from third parties, such as our partners, advertisers, or social media platforms.

## PRIVACY POLICY (continued)

### USE OF INFORMATION

We use the information we collect for the following purposes:

1. To provide, maintain, and improve the Services: We use the information we collect to provide, maintain, and improve the Services, and to develop new features and services.

2. To communicate with you: We may use your information to contact you with newsletters, marketing or promotional materials, or other information that may be of interest to you. You may opt out of receiving these communications at any time by following the unsubscribe instructions provided in the communication or by contacting us as described below.

3. To personalize your experience: We may use the information we collect to personalize your experience on the Services, such as by showing you content that is more relevant to you.

4. To comply with legal obligations: We may use your information as necessary to comply with our legal obligations, such as to respond to a subpoena or to protect the rights, property, or safety of our company, our users, or the public.

### SHARING OF INFORMATION

We may share your information with the following parties:

1. Service providers: We may share your information with third-party service providers who perform services on our behalf, such as hosting, data analysis, payment processing, and customer service. These service providers are required to use your information only as necessary to provide the services we have retained them to perform.

2. Business partners: We may share your information with our business partners, such as advertisers or sponsors, for the purpose of providing you with offers or promotions that may be of interest to you.

3. Legal purposes: We may share your information as necessary to comply with legal obligations, such as to respond to a subpoena or to protect the rights, property, or safety of our company, our users, or the public.

## PRIVACY POLICY (continued)

4. Corporate transactions: If we are involved in a merger, acquisition, or sale of assets, we may share your information with the parties involved in the transaction.

5. With your consent: We may share your information with third parties when we have your consent to do so.

## DATA RETENTION

We will retain your information for as long as your account is active or as needed to provide you with the Services. We will also retain and use your information as necessary to comply with legal obligations, resolve disputes, and enforce our agreements.

## YOUR RIGHTS

You have the following rights in relation to your information:

1. Access: You have the right to request access to the information we hold about you.

2. Correction: You have the right to request that we correct any information that is inaccurate or incomplete.

3. Deletion: You have the right to request that we delete the information we hold about you.

4. Objection: You have the right to object to our processing of your information.

5. Restriction: You have the right to request that we restrict our processing of your information.

6. Portability: You have the right to request that we transfer your information to another party.

You can exercise these rights by contacting us as described below.

## GDPR AND CCPA

If you are a resident of the European Union or California, you have additional rights under the General Data Protection Regulation (GDPR) and the California Consumer Privacy Act (CCPA). These rights include:

**PRIVACY POLICY (continued)**

1. Right to be informed: You have the right to be informed about the collection and use of your personal data.

2. Right of access: You have the right to request access to the personal data we hold about you and to be provided with information about how we use it.

3. Right to rectification: You have the right to request that we correct any personal data that is inaccurate or incomplete.

4. Right to erasure: You have the right to request that we delete your personal data in certain circumstances, such as when it is no longer necessary for the purposes for which it was collected or when you withdraw your consent.

5. Right to restrict processing: You have the right to request that we restrict our processing of your personal data in certain circumstances, such as when you contest the accuracy of the data or when you object to our use of it.

6. Right to data portability: You have the right to request that we transfer your personal data to another party in a format that is commonly used and machine-readable.

7. Right to object: You have the right to object to our processing of your personal data in certain circumstances, such as when we use it for direct marketing purposes.

You can exercise these rights by contacting us as described below.

**CONTACT US**

If you have any questions or concerns about our privacy practices, or if you would like to exercise your rights, please contact us as follows:

[Contact information]

Last updated: [Date]

# A SAMPLE COOKIE POLICY

**Cookie Policy**

Last updated: [Insert date]

**Introduction**

Our website, [Insert website name], uses cookies to improve your user experience and to ensure that our website functions effectively. This Cookie Policy explains what cookies are, how we use them, and the choices you have when it comes to accepting or rejecting cookies. Please read this policy carefully to understand our views and practices regarding cookies and how they may affect you.

By using our website, you are agreeing to the use of cookies as described in this Cookie Policy. If you do not agree with our use of cookies, you should set your browser settings accordingly or not use our website.

**What are cookies?**

Cookies are small pieces of data that are stored on your device (computer, mobile phone, or tablet) when you visit a website. They are widely used to make websites work, or work more efficiently, as well as to provide information to the owners of the website.

There are two main types of cookies:

- Session cookies are temporary cookies that are deleted from your device when you close your browser.

- Persistent cookies are stored on your device until they expire or are deleted by you.

- Cookies may also be classified as first-party cookies (set by the website you are visiting) or third-party cookies (set by a third-party website).

**How do we use cookies?**

We use cookies for a variety of purposes, including:

## Cookie Policy (continued)

- To personalize your experience on our website and remember your preferences, such as language and region.

- To understand how our website is being used and to improve its performance and user experience.

- To track the effectiveness of our marketing campaigns.

- We may also use third-party cookies to help us analyze website traffic and usage patterns. This data is anonymous and is used to help us improve the performance of our website.

### What are your choices regarding cookies?

You can set your browser to accept or reject all, or certain, cookies. You can also set your browser to prompt you each time a cookie is offered, so that you can decide whether to accept it. However, please note that if you choose to reject cookies, you may not be able to use all the features of our website.

You can also use your browser settings to delete cookies that have already been set. Please refer to the instructions provided by your browser for more information.

You can find more information about cookies, including how to see what cookies have been set on your device and how to manage and delete them, at www.allaboutcookies.org.

### Changes to this Cookie Policy

We reserve the right to change this Cookie Policy at any time. Any changes to this Cookie Policy will be posted on this page and, where appropriate, notified to you by email. Please check back frequently to see any updates or changes to this Cookie Policy.

### Contact us

If you have any questions or concerns about our use of cookies, please contact us at [Insert contact information].

Alright, all of that "official" stuff is done! Now, we can continue our journey through the world of application bundle accompaniments. Keep in mind that as you move forward, understanding and adapting to regional conventions, laws, and preferences will be crucial to your software's success.

In the upcoming chapters, we'll dive into topics like intellectual property, bundle formats, updates, refunds, warranties, payment processing, and promotion. Because nothing says "professional" like having all your ducks in a row. Remember, the world of software development is complex, and having the right support system in place can make a world of difference.

So, let's continue our adventure, exploring opportunities to make your application the best it can be!

# Chapter 6.
# Intellectual Property Considerations

In this chapter, we're going to explore the nitty-gritty of IP protection for software, including copyrights, trademarks, and patents. We'll also touch on trade secrets, the unsung hero of IP protection for software companies. Finally, we'll dive into the world of licensing your IP to others, weighing the pros and cons of sharing your genius creations. Buckle up, because understanding these concepts is a must for any developer or business wanting to create and distribute proprietary software.

It's crucial to wrap your head around the intellectual property (IP) considerations involved in creating proprietary software. Topics like copyright, trademark, and patent law might sound dry, but they're more important than a morning cup of coffee. This includes registering your copyright, safeguarding your trade secrets, and licensing your IP to others.

## COPYRIGHTS

Copyright law is like a warm, fuzzy blanket that protects original works of authorship, such as literature, music, and software. When you create proprietary software, you automatically own the copyright to it. It's generally a good idea to register your copyright with the appropriate government agency, just in case someone tries to steal your thunder.

## TRADEMARKS

A trademark is like a secret handshake. It's a word, phrase, symbol, or design that identifies and distinguishes the source of a product or service. If your software has a brand, consider registering a trademark for it. This can help to prevent others from riding your coattails or confusing consumers with a similar brand name.

## PATENT LAW

A patent is a legal monopoly granted by the government for a limited time in exchange for publicly disclosing an invention. There are different types of patents, including utility patents (for new and useful inventions) and design patents (for new, original, and ornamental designs). If your software has a unique and groundbreaking invention, you might be able to obtain a patent for it. You can check and apply for patents in the U.S. through the U.S. Patent Office at www.uspto.gov.

## TRADE SECRETS

Trade secrets are like the secret ingredient in your grandma's famous cookies. They're confidential information that is valuable to a business because it's not generally known to others. This could include things like proprietary algorithms or processes used in your software. It's vital to protect your trade secrets, for instance, by using non-disclosure agreements and secure storage and handling of confidential information.

## LICENSING

Licensing is like giving someone permission to borrow your favorite book. It refers to the process of allowing others to use your IP in exchange for payment or other consideration. This could include licensing your software and other types of IP such as trademarks and patents. Make sure to carefully consider the terms of any licensing agreements, as they can have significant legal and financial implications.

Coming up, you'll find an example template for a proprietary software licensing agreement. This template is like a recipe for a basic proprietary software licensing agreement that covers the terms and conditions for licensing your software. Feel free to sprinkle in extra provisions specific to your business and software, such as confidentiality, indemnification, and dispute resolution clauses.

Here are a few extra ingredients to whip up the perfect proprietary software licensing agreement for ensuring that it's legally enforceable and adequately protects your rights and interests.

❖ **Customize the Agreement to your Needs**: Make sure to tailor the agreement to your specific needs and requirements, adding or removing provisions or modifying terms and conditions to suit your business and software.

❖ **Use Clear & Concise Language**: Write in simple, easy-to-understand language. Avoid legal jargon or technical terms that might leave the other party scratching their head.

❖ **Review the Agreement with a Lawyer**: Before putting the final touches on your agreement, it's a good idea to have a lawyer review it.

**Software Licensing Agreement**

This Software Licensing Agreement (the "Agreement") is a legal agreement between [Name of Licensor] (the "Licensor") and [Name of Licensee] (the "Licensee") for the licensing of the software [Name of Software] (the "Software").

**1. Grant of License.** The Licensor grants to the Licensee a non-exclusive, non-transferable, limited license to use the Software for the following purposes: [Purposes of use, such as personal use, commercial use, educational use, etc.].

**2. License Fee.** The Licensee shall pay to the Licensor a license fee of [Amount] for the use of the Software, payable in [Currency] as follows: [Payment terms, such as upfront payment, payment upon delivery, or payment upon acceptance].

**3. Restrictions.** The Licensee shall not:
(a) Modify, adapt, or translate the Software.
(b) Reverse engineer, decompile, or disassemble the Software.
(c) Sell, rent, lease, or sublicense the Software.
(d) Remove any proprietary notices or labels on the Software.

**4. Intellectual Property Rights.** The Licensor retains all right, title, and interest in and to the Software, including all intellectual property rights. The Licensee shall not claim any ownership rights in the Software.

**5. Termination.** The License shall terminate automatically if the Licensee breaches any of the terms and conditions of the Agreement. Upon termination, the Licensee shall cease all use of the Software and destroy all copies of the Software.

**6. Disclaimer of Warranty.** The Software is provided "as is" without warranty of any kind, either express or implied, including, but not limited to, the implied warranties of merchantability, fitness for a particular purpose, or non-infringement.

**7. Limitation of Liability.** In no event shall the Licensor be liable for any damages, including, but not limited to, direct, indirect, special, incidental, or consequential damages, arising out of the use or inability to use the Software, even if the Licensor has been advised of the possibility of such damages.

**8. Governing Law.** This Agreement shall be governed by and construed in accordance with the laws of the [State/Country].

---

**Software Licensing Agreement (continued)**

**9. Entire Agreement.** This Agreement constitutes the entire agreement between the Licensor and the Licensee and supersedes all prior or contemporaneous understandings or agreements, whether oral or written.

**10. Waiver.** The failure of the Licensor to exercise or enforce any right or provision of this Agreement shall not constitute a waiver of such right or provision.

**11. Severability.** If any provision of this Agreement is found to be invalid or unenforceable, that provision shall be enforced to the maximum extent possible, and the remaining provisions shall remain in full force and effect.

IN WITNESS WHEREOF, the parties have executed this Agreement as of the date and year first above written.

[Name of Licensor] [Name of Licensee]

---

Armed with these tips and this template, you'll be able to craft a proprietary software licensing agreement that defines the terms and conditions for licensing your software clearly, protects your intellectual property rights, manages risk, and ensures that you and the licensee are on the same wavelength.

By now, you should have a solid understanding of the various types of IP protection available for software and how licensing works. Remember, protecting your intellectual property is an essential part of building a successful software business. It's a bit like locking your doors at night – it's just something you need to do to keep your creations safe and sound.

# Chapter 7.
# Distribution & Delivery

Distribution and delivery are the dynamic duo that ensures your hard work and software genius reach the hands of eager customers. In this chapter, we'll navigate the treacherous waters of distribution channels, guide you through the payment processing jungle, and help you avoid the quicksand of subscription handling. Oh, and did we mention we'll also be your trusty sidekick in the realms of software delivery, customer support, refunds, warranties, and other miscellaneous considerations? Buckle up, my friend, because this is going to be one informative and entertaining ride!

## INTRODUCTION TO DISTRIBUTION CHANNELS

Ah, distribution channels - the pathways that lead your software to the promised land of customers' devices. Choose wisely, and you'll find yourself swimming in sales; choose poorly, and you might just end up in the digital doldrums. Fear not, though, because we've got your back. Let's explore some popular distribution channels and their pros and cons, so you can make an informed decision that's right for your software.

### 1. Online Marketplaces:

❖ *Pros:*

> ➢ Access to a vast, diverse audience that's just a click away.
> ➢ Super convenient for customers to purchase and download your software.
> ➢ Often provides marketing and promotional support, so you can focus on what you do best - developing awesome software.

❖ Cons:

> You may need to fork over a commission or fee to the marketplace (boo!).
> Bo prepared to jump through hoops as some marketplaces have strict requirements for listing and selling software.
> Expect some healthy competition from fellow software developers.

## 2. Physical Stores:

❖ Pros:

> Reach those old-school customers who prefer in-person purchases.
> A fantastic opportunity to showcase and demo your software, turning skeptics into believers.
> Sometimes, you'll receive marketing and promotional support.

❖ Cons:

> Your reach may be limited to local or regional customers (unless you go on a worldwide store tour).
> Commission or fees might be part of the deal with physical stores.
> Yep, you guessed it - competition from other developers will be there too.

## 3. Direct to Customers:

❖ Pros:

> Global domination is within your grasp (at least in terms of audience reach)!
> Gain more control over the sales process and customer experience (hello, Captain of Your Own Ship).
> Set your own pricing and terms, without anyone else meddling in your affairs.

❖ Cons:

- ➤ Be prepared to build and maintain your own sales and distribution infrastructure (no small feat!).
- ➤ You'll likely need to invest in significant marketing and promotional efforts.
- ➤ Competition from other developers is still a reality, even when you go solo.

When choosing the optimal distribution channel for your software, consider factors such as your target market, desired pricing and terms, and available resources and infrastructure. Don't be afraid to experiment with different channels or even use multiple channels simultaneously to broaden your reach and rake in more sales. The world of software distribution is your oyster, so go ahead and find your pearl!

In the following sections, we'll dive deeper into the nitty-gritty details of payment processing, subscription handling, software delivery, customer support, refunds, warranties, and other crucial considerations. So stay tuned, and let's continue this thrilling journey together!

## PAYMENT PROCESSING

Money makes the world go 'round, and as a software developer, it's the bread and butter that keeps your creative juices flowing. Let's talk payment processing, the magical act of turning your customers' hard-earned cash into digital funds that you can use to further fuel your software empire. But tread carefully, as not all payment options are created equal! To help you make sense of it all, here's a handy breakdown of some popular choices:

❖ **Credit/Debit Card:**

- ➤ The lowdown: The undisputed king of the payment world, credit and debit cards reign supreme for software purchases.

> ➤ How it works: Partner with a third-party payment processor like Stripe or PayPal to securely handle transactions and encrypt sensitive payment data.

❖ **Mobile Payments:**

> ➤ The lowdown: Ideal for customers who live and breathe through their mobile devices.
> ➤ How it works: Apps like Apple Pay or Google Pay, or even QR codes and NFC tags, make mobile payments a breeze.

❖ **Cryptocurrencies:**

> ➤ The lowdown: Perfect for those who prefer to dabble in digital currencies like Bitcoin.
> ➤ How it works: Accept cryptocurrencies as payment for your software by integrating a crypto payment gateway.

❖ **Direct Debit:**

> ➤ The lowdown: A popular option for recurring payments, such as software subscriptions.
> ➤ How it works: Directly debit the customer's bank account for the purchase amount.

❖ **Wire Transfer:**

> ➤ The lowdown: Works best for large or international payments.
> ➤ How it works: Process payments via bank-to-bank wire transfers.

❖ **Electronic Checks:**

> ➤ The lowdown: The digital cousin of the traditional paper check.
> ➤ How it works: Customers provide their bank account and routing number to make payments electronically.

The key here is to cater to your customers' preferences and offer a variety of payment options, increasing the likelihood of closing the deal. Happy customers equal more sales, after all!

## SUBSCRIPTION HANDLING

So, you've decided to offer your software on a subscription basis – excellent choice! But with great power comes great responsibility, and you'll need a solid system for handling subscriptions. Keep things transparent and user-friendly to keep your customers content and coming back for more. Here's a step-by-step guide to building a subscription handling system that's the bee's knees:

1. **Determine the Terms & Pricing:** Set the duration (monthly, yearly), pricing for each tier, and any extra goodies you want to offer subscribers.

2. **Set Up a Payment Gateway:** Use a payment processor like Stripe or PayPal to handle recurring payments securely and efficiently.

3. **Create a System for Managing Subscriptions:** Implement a customer database or subscription management platform to track subscription status, process upgrades/ downgrades, and handle billing/invoicing.

4. **Communicate Clearly with Subscribers:** Keep subscribers in the loop on terms, benefits, and updates to minimize churn and keep them happy.

5. **Monitor & Optimize:** Regularly review your subscription management system's performance, identify areas for improvement, and tweak as needed.

With a robust system in place, you'll be well on your way to managing your subscription business like a pro and providing top-notch experiences for your customers. So, feel free to conquer the subscription world!

## SOFTWARE DELIVERY

Software delivery – the pièce de résistance of your software-selling journey. This is where the fruits of your labor land in the hands of your eager customers, and it's crucial to make it a smooth and pleasant experience. After all, you wouldn't want a bumpy ride to spoil the grand finale! Fret not, for we've got your back with a breakdown of steps to create a stellar software delivery system.

### DETERMINE THE DELIVERY METHOD

First things first, pick the best way to get your software into your customers' hands. Here are your contenders:

❖ Downloadable from your website

❖ License key to unlock the software

❖ Physically shipped CD or USB drive

### SET UP A SYSTEM FOR DELIVERING THE SOFTWARE

Now that you've chosen your champion, it's time to build a system that ensures a seamless delivery. Let's explore our options…

Once upon a time, in the land of software development, you, the valiant creator, have chosen your champion – the method of delivering your masterpiece to the eager hands of your users. But the journey doesn't end there. No, the path ahead requires more than mere choice; it demands the crafting of a seamless delivery system, one that ensures your users' experience is nothing short of magical.

In this thrilling tale, we'll explore the two methods of software delivery – Website Delivery and License Key Delivery.

Our adventure begins with Website Delivery, where our hero embarks on a quest to find a reliable website or file hosting service that offers ample bandwidth and storage for large downloads. Armed with the perfect hosting partner, our hero crafts a user-friendly download page, complete with clear instructions and any requirements or restrictions that users may encounter.

With the stage set, our hero must now implement a system to track and manage downloads, processing returns or exchanges, and handling customer support – a customer database or order management platform fit for a king. Communication is key in this quest, as our hero must keep their loyal subjects (customers) informed about the download process, from the mystical URL to the estimated time and any requirements they might face.

But hark! Another hero emerges in the form of License Key Delivery. In this epic, our champion must first determine their ideal licensing model, choosing between per-user, per-machine, or subscription-based licensing. Once chosen, the hero sets up a system for creating unique keys for each customer and storing and managing them in a treasure trove of data.

To activate and manage these coveted licenses, our hero implements a powerful tool – a customer database or license management platform – to track license status, process upgrades or downgrades, and handle customer support. Communication remains vital, as our hero keeps customers informed about the licensing process, from obtaining and activating keys to understanding license terms and any requirements.

In the end, both heroes prevail, ensuring that your software delivery system is a tale of triumph, with an audience of happy users to boot.

Well, that was fun! So, in the end, choose the method that is right for you. Just think about your product and your customers, and be sure to choose the method that suites them best!

### TRACK & MANAGE DELIVERIES

Establish a system for tracking and managing deliveries, such as a customer database or order management platform. This system should handle order status, returns/exchanges, and customer support.

## COMMUNICATE CLEARLY WITH CUSTOMERS

Make the delivery process crystal clear, including delivery method, estimated time, and any requirements or restrictions. A smooth customer experience is the name of the game!

With a top-notch software delivery system in place, you'll be well-equipped to delight your customers and showcase your amazing software. Now go forth and let your digital masterpieces fly!

## A REAL-WORLD EXAMPLE

Let's bring it all together with an example: You've built your software, created a website, and chosen devpi as your package management system and Stripe as your payment system. Here's how to set up your website for hosting, selling, and distributing your software:

1. **Install & Configure devpi:** Follow the instructions to set up your package repository.

2. **Create & Package your Software:** Define package metadata in a setup.py file, specify files in a MANIFEST.in file, and use the devpi tool to create a package and upload it to your repository.

3. **Set Up your Website & Payment System:** Integrate your website with Stripe and devpi, and create a web page that provides purchasing and downloading information.

4. **Test & Deploy your System:** Make sure everything is working correctly before making your software available to the public. Don't forget to market and promote your software!

Remember to consider updates, support, and legal and financial aspects. Seek advice from professionals to ensure you're covering all bases, and you'll be well on your way to running a successful software business!

## CUSTOMER SUPPORT

To avoid any software-related meltdowns, providing top-notch customer support is crucial. Imagine a world where your customers can reach out to you and get help when they need it, all while you're lounging by the pool. By managing customer inquiries effectively and providing top-quality experiences, you'll make it a breeze for customers to contact you and get the help they need. So, let's dive into the steps to set up a customer support system that's as smooth as butter.

1. **Choose Your Channels:** Pick your customer support channels, whether it's email, phone, chat, or even carrier pigeon (we recommend something more modern, though). Think about what's convenient for your customers and fits within your resources.

2. **Inquiry Management System:** Create a customer inquiry management system like a customer service platform or a good ol' spreadsheet. Make sure it can track, prioritize, and assign inquiries to the right people.

3. **Technical Support:** Set up resources like a knowledge base, FAQs, or a support forum. You could also assemble a team of technical support superheroes to handle the trickier questions.

4. **Returns & Refunds:** Establish a system for handling returns and refunds, complete with policies and a smooth process. Remember to communicate these policies clearly and be fair when processing requests.

## REFUNDS & WARRANTIES

As a software developer, it's important to think about your legal obligations, even if it's not as exciting as designing the next killer app. While you're not required to offer a refund policy or warranty, it's good practice to do so to build trust in your product.

A refund policy offers protection to users who are not satisfied with your software, while a warranty provides assurance that your software will perform as intended and be free from defects.

## WARRANTIES

Warranties can serve different purposes, such as limiting your liability or providing assurance to your customers. You might want to consult a lawyer to determine the best type of warranty for your software license or EULA.

Below are some sample warranty examples you may want to consider familiarizing yourself with.

### SAMPLE WARRANTY #1:

---

**Warranty**

[Product Name] is provided "as is" and without any warranties, express or implied. [Company Name] specifically disclaims any implied warranties of merchantability, fitness for a particular purpose, or non-infringement. [Company Name] shall not be liable for any damages whatsoever, including but not limited to, direct, indirect, special, incidental, or consequential damages, arising out of or in connection with the use of [Product Name].

---

## SAMPLE WARRANTY #2:

**Warranty**

[Product Name] is warranted to be free from defects in materials and workmanship for a period of [X] months from the date of purchase.

If a defect arises during the warranty period, [Company Name] will, at its option, repair or replace the product. This warranty does not cover damages caused by accident, misuse, or unauthorized modification.

To make a warranty claim, please contact us at [Contact Email] and provide your order number and a detailed explanation of the issue you are experiencing.

[Company Name] does not offer any additional warranties beyond the one stated above.

In designing and implementing a warranty for your software, it is important to consider:

❖ **The Length of the Warranty Period:** You should consider the expected lifespan of your software and offer a warranty period that is appropriate.

❖ **The Types of Issues Covered by the Warranty:** It is important to be clear about the types of defects that are covered by the warranty, such as defects in materials and workmanship. You may also want to specify that the warranty does not cover damages caused by accidents, misuse, or unauthorized modification.

❖ **The Process for Making a Warranty Claim:** Make sure to provide a clear and easy-to-use process for customers to make a warranty claim, such as an email address or online form. It is also a good idea to include an order number to help you track and process warranty claims efficiently.

❖ **Any Additional Warranties Offered:** You may choose to offer additional warranties beyond the basics, such as a longer warranty period or coverage for certain types of damages. Make sure to clearly communicate any additional warranties you offer to your customers.

## REFUNDS

Let's talk about refunds for different distribution methods: digital and physical. The process will vary depending on how you're delivering your software. For digitally distributed software, think about:

➢ The refund request period
➢ The refund request process
➢ The criteria for granting a refund
➢ Exceptions or exclusions
➢ Limitations on liability

---

**Refund Policy**

At [Company Name], we strive to provide high-quality software products that meet the needs and expectations of our customers. However, we understand that there may be circumstances where a customer is not satisfied with their purchase.

If you are not satisfied with your purchase of one of our software products, you may be eligible for a refund within [X] days of your purchase. To request a refund, please contact our customer support team at [contact email] with your purchase receipt and a brief explanation of why you are requesting a refund.

We will review each refund request on a case-by-case basis and make a determination based on the specific circumstances of the request. Please note that we reserve the right to deny a refund request if it is deemed to be made in bad faith or for reasons that are not in line with the terms of this refund policy.

---

For physically distributed software, you'll need to consider similar factors, but account for the added complexity of physical distribution. So, next we'll look at a sample refund policy for physically distributed software.

## Refund Policy

Our policy lasts [insert time period, e.g., 30 days]. If [insert time period] has passed since your purchase, unfortunately we can't offer you a refund or exchange.

To be eligible for a return, your software must be unused and in the same condition that you received it. It must also be in the original packaging.

To complete your return, we require a receipt or proof of purchase.

Please do not send your purchase back to the manufacturer.

There are certain situations where only partial refunds are granted (if applicable):

- Any item not in its original condition, is damaged or missing parts for reasons not due to our error

- Any item that is returned more than [insert time period] after delivery

### Refunds (If Applicable)

Once your return is received and inspected, we will send you an email to notify you that we have received your returned item. We will also notify you of the approval or rejection of your refund.

If you are approved, then your refund will be processed, and a credit will automatically be applied to your credit card or original method of payment, within a certain amount of days.

### Late or Missing Refunds (If Applicable)

If you haven't received a refund yet, first check your bank account again.

Then contact your credit card company, it may take some time before your refund is officially posted.

Next contact your bank. There is often some processing time before a refund is posted.

If you've done all of this and you still have not received your refund yet, please contact us at [insert contact information].

**Refund Policy (continued)**

**Sale Items** (If Applicable)

Only regular priced items may be refunded, unfortunately sale items cannot be refunded.

**Exchanges** (If Applicable)

We only replace items if they are defective or damaged. If you need to exchange it for the same item, send us an email at [insert contact information] and send your item to [insert address].

**Gifts**

If the item was marked as a gift when purchased and shipped directly to you, you'll receive a gift credit for the value of your return. Once the returned item is received, a gift certificate will be mailed to you.

If the item wasn't marked as a gift when purchased, or the gift giver had the order shipped to themselves to give to you later, we will send a refund to the gift giver, and they will find out about your return.

**Shipping**

To return your product, you should mail your product to: [insert address]

You will be responsible for paying for your own shipping costs for returning your item. Shipping costs are non-refundable. If you receive a refund, the cost of return shipping will be deducted from your refund.

Depending on where you live, the time it may take for your exchanged product to reach you, may vary.

If you are shipping an item over $75, you should consider using a trackable shipping service or purchasing shipping insurance. We don't guarantee that we will receive your returned item.

## ADDITIONAL CONSIDERATIONS

Don't forget about the other factors that could impact your software distribution and delivery, like taxes, shipping costs, and international distribution. It's important to cover all your bases and ensure a smooth experience for your customers. After all, nobody wants to pay unexpected fees or wait forever for their software to arrive. So, make sure you consider every aspect of distribution and delivery to keep your customers happy and coming back for more!

# Chapter 8.
# Handling Updates

In today's digital world, keeping your software fresh and updated is as vital as keeping your milk from turning sour. Nobody wants to be caught with a stale application or a chunky glass of milk, right? In this chapter, we'll dive into the thrilling world of software updates, exploring different approaches and offering some spicy tips to keep your users coming back for more.

But before we dig into the various update strategies, let's go over a few key considerations that you should keep in mind when creating a system for distributing updates to a commercial application:

❖ **Make sure your application can be updated easily**: Ensure your application can be updated without causing disruptions to the user. This may involve creating an update system that can run automatically in the background or providing users with an easy way to install updates manually.

❖ **Communicate updates to users**: Keep users informed about updates to your application. This may involve sending notifications or emails when updates are available, or providing information about updates in your application's user interface.

❖ **Test updates thoroughly**: Make sure to test updates to your application to ensure they are stable and don't introduce any new problems. This may involve testing updates on various systems and configurations.

❖ **Consider the impact of updates on users**: When planning updates, think about their potential impact on users. This may involve preserving user data and settings during updates or providing users with tools to migrate their data to new versions of the application.

❖ **Plan for handling update failures**: Have a plan in place for handling update failures or rollbacks. This may involve providing users with a way to revert to an earlier version of the application if necessary or having a process in place for addressing update-related issues.

With these considerations in mind, you're ready to create a reliable, user-friendly update system that minimizes disruptions to your users.

Now, let's proceed to explore the different approaches to providing software updates, ensuring you can make the best choice for your software's flavor profile.

## COMMON UPDATE APPROACHES

Imagine you've crafted the perfect software masterpiece, but let's face it, nobody's perfect. Just like your favorite pizza joint keeps updating their menu, your software needs a refresh too. This could mean adding mouthwatering new features, squashing pesky bugs, or tossing in some extra security toppings. So, let's discuss a few different approaches you could take to creating updates for your application. To make things more deliciously specific, we'll use a Python application as our example.

### THE FULL MAKEOVER: NEW VERSION FOR EACH UPDATE

You could treat your software like a fashionista, creating a brand new version for each update. Here, you'd set up a new project directory for every update, copy the relevant files from the old directory, and then strut your development prowess in the new directory. Ready to release the update? Package the snazzy new version and distribute it to your adoring users.

## THE ORGANIZED APPROACH: VERSION CONTROL

Or, you could be the Marie Kondo of software updates and use version control software, such as Git, to keep everything neat and tidy. Create a new branch for each update, make your code changes in the new branch, and then merge them back into the main branch when you're ready to release the update. Not only will this spark joy in your code, but it also makes it easier to roll back changes if necessary.

## THE SMOOTH OPERATOR: PACKAGE MANAGEMENT SYSTEM

If you're the type who enjoys a well-oiled machine, consider using a package management system like PyPI to manage updates to your application. Create a package for your application and then distribute updates to users by uploading new versions of the package to the system. This can make it easier to distribute updates and ensure that users can install the latest version of your application without breaking a sweat.

Keep in mind, there is no one "best" way to create updates for a Python application, and the approach you choose will depend on your specific needs and preferences. Much like choosing between pineapple or anchovies on your pizza, it's a matter of taste. In the upcoming sections, we'll delve into the considerations for different approaches, a general approach to updates, and additional update considerations, ensuring you can make the best choice for your software's flavor profile.

## CONSIDERATIONS FOR DIFFERENT APPROACHES

When choosing an update approach, picture yourself as a contestant on a game show where the grand prize is user satisfaction. Just like in any game show, there are a few factors to juggle, such as the frequency of updates, the size and scope of the updates, and their impact on your users. Take your time and weigh your options, because the right choice can lead to a standing ovation from your user base.

Let's revisit the three update approaches mentioned earlier, exploring them as if they were contestants on our imaginary game show:

1. **Creating a New Version of the Application for Each Update**: In this approach, each update would replace the entire application on the user's computer, requiring them to reinstall the whole shebang. This option can be a bit cumbersome and might lead to a few eye rolls from your users.

2. **Using Version Control to Manage Updates**: This approach involves making changes to the codebase and distributing the updated code to users. Depending on the implementation, the update may or may not replace the entire application on the user's computer. While more efficient, it still requires some careful planning.

3. **Using a Package Management System**: With this method, updates involve distributing a new version of the package to users. The package management system handles the installation and any necessary dependencies. The update may or may not replace the entire application on the user's computer, depending on the implementation. This option might just be the crowd-pleaser you're looking for.

When deciding on an update approach, consider your users' needs and your application's complexity. You may even want to offer options, such as automatic or manual updates, to cater to different preferences.

## A GENERAL APPROACH TO UPDATES

Let's dive into a one-size-fits-most approach to handling updates, kind of like a snuggly blanket that keeps everyone warm and toasty:

❖ Build a periodic call to your website within the software that checks for updates and notifies the user.

❖ Prompt the user to install the update, allowing the application to download and install it from the website.

❖ Include a testing mechanism to check the update's success after installation.

❖ In case of update failure or undesired changes, allow users to revert to the previous version through an application menu option.

❖ Offer an in-app feedback mechanism for users to report on update successes or failures.

While this approach covers many key considerations, there are additional points that are worth bearing in mind.

Consider offering multiple update channels. Providing a "stable" channel for users seeking reliability and a "beta" channel for those wanting to test new features can cater to different user preferences.

It's important to provide clear installation instructions. Minimize update-related issues by offering detailed instructions or video tutorials, ensuring that users can easily navigate the update process.

Don't forget to communicate the benefits of each update. Highlight new features or improvements to encourage users to install updates and build trust in your product.

Finally, plan for handling update-related issues. Provide a way for users to report issues and offer timely support to help them resolve any problems they encounter.

Remember to routinely review and refine your update process, and you'll have a user-friendly update system that earns rave reviews from your users!

## ADDITIONAL UPDATE CONSIDERATIONS

When it comes to handling updates, there's always room for a little extra pizzazz. Depending on your business and software, you might need to consider factors like backward compatibility, user testing, or the impact of updates on third-party integrations. Just like an encore performance, the show isn't over until you've covered all the bases and left your audience wanting more.

# Chapter 9.
# Marketing & Promotion

Let's dive into the world of marketing and promotion, the lifeblood of your software's success. Remember, even the most genius of software won't sell if nobody knows about it. Picture yourself in a virtual megaphone-wielding mode, ready to tell the world about your digital creation. In this chapter, we'll guide you through some savvy strategies to get your software in front of the right people, including cozying up to influencers, navigating the wild west of legalities, and compensating your promoters with more than just a pat on the back. Ready? Let's go!

## AN INTRODUCTION TO MARKETING & PROMOTION

Ah, influencers. Love 'em or hate 'em, they can be the golden ticket to promoting your software. In this chapter, we'll dive into how to leverage their massive followings and hypnotic persuasion powers to help your software reach the heights of digital stardom. We've got a lot to cover, but we'll switch up our tactics along the way to keep things fresh, interesting, and—most importantly—useful for you. So, let's kick things off with a look at the power of influencers.

## INFLUENCERS AS PROMOTERS

Influencer marketing is like a modern-day, digital version of celebrity endorsements. Picture your software on the metaphorical arm of the most popular person in school. Sounds appealing, right? Let's break down the process of finding, approaching, and negotiating with these social media dynamos.

## FINDING SOCIAL MEDIA INFLUENCERS

Before you can collaborate with an influencer, you need to find the right one. Here are some ways to do that:

❖ **Research & Identify Influencers in Your Industry or Target Market:** Look for influencers with a large following in your software's niche. You want someone who's known for promoting relevant products and services. Social media platforms, search engines, and industry publications can help you find these digital gems.

❖ **Use Influencer Marketing Platforms:** Plenty of platforms exist to help you connect with influencers and negotiate promotional campaigns. These platforms often have tools to search for influencers based on location, audience size, engagement rate, and other criteria. They also let you compare the cost and effectiveness of different influencers, making your life a whole lot easier.

❖ **Reach Out to Influencers Directly:** If you're feeling bold, reach out to influencers directly. Send them a message or email introducing yourself and your software, and ask if they'd be interested in promoting it.

## APPROACHING & NEGOTIATING WITH INFLUENCERS

Once you've found your dream influencer, it's time to make your pitch. But, how do you do that?

Before you even think about reaching out, do your homework. Start by researching the influencer & their audience. Understand the influencer's audience and the type of content they create. This will help you craft a pitch that speaks their language.

When you do make contact, be upfront about what you're asking for and what you're offering in return. Ensure that you're clear & concise! Tell them about your software, its benefits, and the kind of promotion you're looking for.

Also, influencers might have their own ideas and suggestions for a promotional campaign, so be flexible & open to negotiation: . Be open to discussing different options and finding a mutually beneficial arrangement. Remember, flexibility is key to a successful collaboration.

## COMPENSATING INFLUENCERS

Now, let's talk money—or other forms of compensation. It rare that anyone is willing to promote a product for free, so we should discuss a few ways to reward influencers for promoting your software.

Payment is always a welcome reward. You can pay influencers a flat fee for a one-time promotion, or a recurring fee for ongoing promotion. Keep in mind, though, that top influencers can command hefty fees.

If payment isn't right for you, you could offer something other than money. Offering your software or a related service in exchange for promotion can be a win-win. Influencers may be more interested in trying out or testing your product, which can help build a longer-lasting relationship beyond a single promotional campaign.

Of course, there is always commissions, too. Tying compensation to the sales or referrals generated by an influencer can be a great motivator. By offering a commission, you align your interests with theirs, ensuring they're as invested in your software's success as you are.

These popular options are just the tip of the iceberg when it comes to marketing and promoting your software. So, we'll dive deeper into influencer marketing platforms, legalities and regulations of paid promotion, compensating promoters, commission structures, contracts, marketing materials, and more coming up! By the end of this chapter, you'll have a well-rounded understanding of how to make your software the talk of the digital town. So, buckle up and enjoy the ride!

## INFLUENCER MARKETING PLATFORMS

As you embark on your influencer marketing journey, you'll be thrilled to know that there are plenty of platforms to help you find and collaborate with influencers. These platforms are your gateway to connecting with influencers who are as eager to promote your software as you are to have it promoted. Here are a few noteworthy ones:

❖ **InfluencerDB:** This platform specializes in helping you find influencers on Instagram, YouTube, and TikTok. With its tools, you can search for influencers based on audience size, engagement rate, and location. Plus, it helps you manage and track promotional campaigns.

❖ **Upfluence:** Upfluence covers a broader spectrum of social media platforms, including Instagram, Twitter, and YouTube. It offers similar tools for influencer search, campaign management, and tracking.

❖ **AspireIQ:** Another platform for Instagram and YouTube influencers, AspireIQ helps you find the perfect influencer for your campaign based on various criteria, and also provides management and tracking features.

❖ **BrandSnob:** Focusing on Instagram and TikTok influencers, BrandSnob has all the tools you need to find, manage, and track the ideal influencer for your software promotion.

To get started with these platforms, create an account and use their search tools to find influencers that align with your criteria. Many platforms also offer analytics and reporting tools, so you can track your campaign's performance and measure the ROI of your influencer marketing efforts.

## THE LEGALITIES & REGULATIONS OF PAID PROMOTION

Now, let's talk about the not-so-fun (but very important) stuff: legalities and regulations. When working with influencers, it's crucial to be aware of disclosure requirements, endorsement guidelines, and rules related to paid promotions. Don't worry, we've got you covered:

❖ **Disclosure:** Many jurisdictions require you to disclose your relationship with the influencer. This includes mentioning that the influencer is being compensated for promoting your software and providing information about the terms of the compensation.

❖ **Endorsement Guidelines:** Social media platforms like Instagram and Twitter have their own guidelines for disclosing sponsored content and paid endorsements. Be sure to review these guidelines and ensure compliance when working with influencers.

❖ **Advertising Laws:** Familiarize yourself with the laws and regulations governing advertising and marketing practices, including those related to deceptive advertising and the use of endorsements and testimonials.

To ensure compliance, consider seeking legal advice, reviewing industry best practices, and implementing policies and procedures. You may also want to obtain consent or disclosures from the influencer's followers and have a process for tracking and documenting your compliance efforts. After all, it's better to be safe than sorry!

## COMPENSATING PROMOTERS

Let's dive into the world of compensating influencers for their hard work promoting your software. You can opt for monetary payments, free products or services, or commissions based on sales generated. It's crucial to choose the right approach for your business and budget and communicate the terms clearly to the influencer.

Some platforms allow you to compensate influencers through commissions, which can effectively align their interests with yours. However, not all platforms offer this option, and terms may vary. Always review terms and conditions and negotiate directly with the influencer.

And don't forget about the legal and regulatory requirements for compensating influencers through commissions. Stay compliant with all relevant laws and regulations, including disclosing your relationship with the influencer and obtaining any necessary consent or disclosures from their followers.

## PAYING COMMISSIONS

Commissions are a popular way to compensate influencers or promoters. To create a successful commission-based relationship, consider these strategies:

- ❖ **Commission Rate:** Factors like product cost, influencer's target audience, and expected ROI will impact the commission rate. Offer higher commission rates for influencers with larger, more engaged audiences or for products with higher profit margins.

- ❖ **Tracking & Measurement:** Implement a system for tracking sales or referrals generated by the influencer, such as unique tracking links or coupons.

- ❖ **Payment Terms:** Determine the frequency and method of payment, whether it's monthly, a lump sum after the campaign, or using a payment service like PayPal.

- ❖ **Contract Terms:** Outline the terms of the commission arrangement in a written contract to protect both parties and ensure a clear understanding of the agreement.

## COMMISSION CONTRACTS

A legally binding agreement is essential when offering commissions to influencers. A commission contract should specify terms such as percentage of sales, duration of the agreement, and other relevant details.

Let's look at a simple list of the common provisions for a commission contract.

1. **Parties:** Clearly identify the parties involved in the agreement, including the business (you) and the influencer.

2. **Scope of Work:** Detail the influencer's promotional responsibilities and the specific products or services they'll promote.

3. **Commission Rate:** Define the commission rate as a percentage of sales generated by the influencer.

4. **Tracking & Measurement:** Explain how sales or referrals will be tracked and measured, including any tools or unique tracking links.

5. **Payment Terms:** Specify payment frequency, payment method, and any payment thresholds.

6. **Duration & Termination:** Establish the duration of the agreement and the conditions under which it can be terminated.

7. **Confidentiality:** Include a confidentiality clause to protect sensitive information related to the business and the influencer.

8. **Governing Law & Jurisdiction:** Determine the governing law and jurisdiction that will apply to any disputes arising from the agreement.

9. **Indemnification:** Define the terms of indemnification to protect both parties from potential liabilities.

10. **Amendments & Waivers:** Set the conditions for amending or waiving any provisions of the agreement.

Written out, this should look something like the document below, which you can use when hiring an influencer to promote your products or applications. Just remember, this is just a starting point. You should tailor your contract to your specific needs and consult with a legal professional to ensure it covers all of your necessary aspects.

**[Date]**

This Commission Contract ("Agreement") is made and entered into by and between [Your Company], with a business address of [Address], and [Influencer], with a business address of [Address] (collectively referred to as the "Parties").

**Purpose:** The purpose of this Agreement is to set forth the terms and conditions under which [Influencer] will promote [Your Company]'s products or applications ("Products") through [Influencer]'s social media channels ("Channels").

**Term:** This Agreement shall commence on [Date] and shall continue until [Date] or until terminated by either Party upon thirty (30) days written notice.

**Commission:** In consideration for the promotion of the Products through the Channels, [Your Company] shall pay [Influencer] a commission of [Percentage] of the sales or referrals generated through the Channels. The commission shall be paid on a [Monthly/Lump Sum] basis, and payment shall be made through [Payment Method].

**Tracking and Measurement:** [Your Company] shall provide [Influencer] with unique tracking links or coupons that shall be used to promote the Products through the Channels. [Your Company] shall track the sales or referrals generated through these links and shall pay the commission to [Influencer] based on these tracked metrics.

**Termination:** This Agreement may be terminated by either Party upon thirty (30) days written notice if the other Party breaches any material term or condition of this Agreement.

**Governing Law:** This Agreement shall be governed by and construed in accordance with the laws of the State of [State].

**Entire Agreement:** This Agreement constitutes the entire agreement between the Parties, and supersedes all prior agreements or understandings, whether oral or written.

IN WITNESS WHEREOF, the Parties have executed this Agreement as of the date and year first above written.

[Your Company]

[Influencer]

## MARKETING MATERIALS FOR RUNNING A PROMOTION

Welcome to the world of marketing materials! These resources, like brochures, flyers, website banners, and social media posts, are essential in promoting your software. Let's explore the minimum viable materials you need to effectively market your software.

Check out this list of must-haves before launching your promotional campaign:

❖ **Website or Online Platform:** Users need a place to learn about your app, its features, benefits, and how to purchase it.

❖ **Product Description:** Explain what your app does, who it's for, and what sets it apart from similar products.

❖ **Screenshots or Videos:** Show off your app's features and functionality.

❖ **Customer Reviews or Testimonials:** Offer evidence of your app's effectiveness and value.

❖ **Pricing Page:** Share the cost of your app and any available discounts or promotions.

❖ **Call to Action:** Encourage users to purchase or download your app.

When working with an influencer or other promoter, consider providing additional materials like:

❖ **Product Sample or Demo:** Allow influencers to try your app and give authentic reviews or testimonials.

❖ **Media Kit:** Include high-quality images, videos, press releases, or news articles about your app.

❖ **Key Messages or Talking Points:** Highlight the unique features and benefits of your app.

❖ **Detailed Brief or Guidelines:** Outline the campaign's goals, objectives, and specific messaging or content for the influencer to focus on.

❖ **Target Audience Demographics and Interests:** Help the influencer tailor their promotion to the most relevant and engaged followers.

## ADDITIONAL MARKETING CONSIDERATIONS

When it comes to marketing and promoting your software, you might encounter additional factors depending on your business and goals. We'll end this chapter with some extra elements to think about as you develop your marketing and promotion strategy. With these marketing materials and considerations in mind, you'll be well-equipped to launch a successful promotional campaign and make a splash in the world of software!

❖ **Targeting Specific Demographics:** Ensure your marketing efforts reach the right audience by identifying and targeting specific demographics.

❖ **Paid Advertising:** Consider using paid advertising on social media or search engines to boost your app's visibility and reach.

❖ **Measuring Effectiveness:** Continuously monitor and measure the effectiveness of your promotion efforts through analytics, conversion rates, and other metrics to optimize your strategy.

# Chapter 10.
# Navigating Legalities and Automation Magic: The Grand Finale!

As we approach the end of this thrilling journey through the world of software commercialization, let's gather our legal know-how and sprinkle some automation magic onto the process. We'll discuss distributor liability, licensing, permitting, and other essential considerations, while also exploring tools and techniques that can help you automate and streamline your software distribution. This way, you'll be well-equipped to tackle the exciting world of software distribution, leaving the book with a strong, memorable impression.

## WALKING THE LEGAL TIGHTROPE:
### DISTRIBUTOR LIABILITY AND LICENSING

Entering the world of software distribution can feel like stepping onto a legal tightrope. Balancing your responsibilities as a software distributor is crucial to protect both yourself and your users. Start by understanding your legal obligations, researching specific licenses or permits, and seeking professional advice when needed. Being transparent with users and including disclaimers and limitations of liability in your terms of use will help you navigate the legal labyrinth.

## THE FINE PRINT:
### TAXES, SHIPPING, AND INDUSTRY REGULATIONS

While exploring the finer points of software distribution, don't forget about the additional considerations that can impact your journey. From understanding tax requirements to factoring in shipping costs for physical copies, there's plenty to keep in mind. Stay aware of international legal requirements, cultural differences, and industry regulations to ensure your software complies with standards and reaches as wide an audience as possible. And always prioritize maintaining a positive reputation by addressing customer concerns and providing excellent support.

## SPRINKLING AUTOMATION MAGIC: STREAMLINING YOUR SOFTWARE DISTRIBUTION

Now that we've explored the legal side of things, let's sprinkle some automation magic on the process to make your life easier. Embrace project management tools like Asana or Trello to keep your team on track, and use version control systems like Git for effective collaboration. Automate code building and testing with CI servers, and simplify software dependencies with package managers.

But the automation doesn't stop there. Embrace tools and technologies to distribute your software effortlessly, scale it using cloud platforms, and manage updates. Automate payments and subscriptions, set up an online store, and streamline customer interactions and support using CRM systems and customer support platforms. Finally, track and resolve software issues effectively with bug tracking systems to continuously improve your product's quality.

And there you have it! By thoroughly understanding and addressing various legal considerations and embracing automation tools, you'll be well-prepared to face the challenges of software distribution. So, go forth and conquer the software world with your incredible creations!

Closing the book on this adventure, remember that the possibilities are endless, and the world is eagerly waiting for your next big idea. The road may not always be smooth, but armed with the knowledge and tools we've discussed, you're now ready to turn your hobby into a thriving business. So, take a deep breath, step out with confidence, and make your mark on the software industry. Good luck, and happy coding!

# Afterword

As we bid adieu to this thrilling adventure, I hope you've gained some priceless nuggets of wisdom for the journey ahead. Trust me, I've been in your shoes, pondering the same questions and wishing for a straightforward guide like the one you've just read. But remember, the learning doesn't stop here. With the process, considerations, and options at your fingertips, you can now craft your very own strategies to conquer the world of software monetization.

Throughout this book, I've sprinkled some specific examples from my own experiences. For instance, I've mentioned using Python, PyPI, and devpi in the realm of development. But worry not, these are merely the tools that populated my personal toolbox. I'm well aware that countless other solutions are out there, ripe for the picking. So, consider my examples as mere illustrations, not strict prescriptions—allowing you to confidently choose the perfect tools for your unique endeavors.

As you venture forth, I hope you're feeling pumped and ready to monetize your development efforts, not just as a hobbyist or an employee, but as a trailblazing entrepreneur. You, my friend, are a cauldron of brilliant ideas waiting to be unleashed upon the world. Whether you're simplifying a task, solving a problem, or filling a societal gap, I'm confident that you'll make a lasting impact.

If there's just one gem of knowledge from this book that helps you turn your dream into reality, then I'm honored to have been your guide on this exciting journey. So, put on your coding cape, and with luck and determination as your trusty sidekicks, go forth and conquer!

www.ingramcontent.com/pod-product-compliance
Lightning Source LLC
LaVergne TN
LVHW051746050326
832903LV00029B/2750